INFINITE
ABILITIES

Living Your Life on Purpose

A Story

D1400310

INFINITE ABILITIES

Living Your Life on Purpose

A Story

IVY HELSTEIN

Oakhill Press
Greensboro, NC

This publication is designed to provide accurate and authoritative information in regard to the subject matter covered. It is sold with the understanding that the publisher is not engaged in rendering legal, accounting, or other professional service. If legal advice or other expert assistance is required, the services of a competent professional person should be sought. *From a Declaration of Principles jointly adopted by a committee of the American Bar Association and a committee of Publishers.*

10   9   8   7   6   5   4   3   2   1

Library of Congress Cataloging in Publication Data

Communication Dynamics
    Infinite abilities : living your life on purpose : a story / by Ivy Helstein
        p. cm.
            ISBN 0-9709015-0-X
        I. Title.
    PS3558.E4777   1998
    813' .54 --dc21   98-50284
                                                                CIP

DEDICATION

To my children, Eden, Flyn, and Hilary, my role models for courage, who gave me unconditional love and support. And to my mother and father, whose experiences with me made this journey possible.

CONTENTS

PREFACE

Right now, as I am writing this preface, I am experiencing all the psychological and emotional and physical symptoms that a significant ending and a new beginning bring. I have procrastinated: gotten up to eat junk food, gone to the bank, wrapped a package, have free-floating anxiety, and made two trips to the bathroom. However, with all that going on, I am still writing and have not permitted my "stuff" to stop me, although I am dying to give in.

All the behavior I just described in embarrassing detail is what prompted me to write this book.

What I discovered through my years of conducting various personal growth workshops and business seminars and counseling private clients, was that regardless of the culture, background, professional status, or gender, the one thing that everyone had in common was their resistance to emotionally separating from their family of origin. And no differently than myself, they were holding on in all kinds of amazing ways so that they wouldn't outgrow and have to leave their old place in the family.

And when I asked, "What do you want most?" the responses invariably were a great loving relationship, money, fame, recognition—personal satisfaction and gratification in some way. Yet, even those that did achieve success in one area by society's standards somehow sabotaged their lives or held themselves back in some other way. And what I found is that the areas that they held themselves back in the most were the very ones that they wanted more than anything. And what they used to stop this "leaving the nest" were an incredible assortment of self-limiting and personally destructive behaviors: addictions, anger, anxiety, guilt, depression, caretaking, shyness, obsessions, financial and other deprivations, bad or no relationships, phobias, abuse, a variety of fears, illnesses, procrastination, and so forth. I could go on and on, from the obvious to the subtle.

And the saddest part, even though they wanted more and better, they kept the old pain and victimizing going. Only now, they were either creating it themselves, still letting the same family keep it going, or finding new people to keep them in their old place.

However, I knew that their desire to change was stronger than their desire to remain the same because they tenaciously kept coming for more help and for more answers, week after week. For some, year after year. I loved and admired them all for their courage, and vowed to give them whatever guidance they needed.

That is why I titled my book *Infinite Abilities*. It was to honor all of these people, and all the ones I have never met, who have so much ability and talent inside. More than anything I needed to reach that scared, unique little child in all of them, and to show them the way. To be Geula—to be that special someone for them.

Most important, I wanted to give them the insights and the step-by-step lessons that would allow them to change—that would allow them to begin their journey that is their true life under their own steam—using their innate power, strengths and resources.

And now that I have explained my motivation for writing this book, or more accurately my purpose for being here, I want to turn my attention personally to you, the man or woman who right now is reading this preface and hopefully will continue reading the book. I want you to know that there are no "together" people . . . never were, never will be. You, me, the CEO in the big corporate office, we are all resistant little children inside in some way, regardless of how we appear or the facades we show to the world. We are all sad, facing some ending, and scared of the unknown and the new beginning. We even feel undeserving of the excitement and potential and happiness that lie ahead in some area of our lives.

It is very important that you know you are not alone. Everyone on the planet now, in the past, and into the future is taking his or her own journey along with you.

Geula says, "We are constantly being sent guidance. All we need to do is tune into the messages."

So begin your new journey, open all your "information receivers"—your ears, eyes, mind, and heart.

Go for it, and trust . . . the best is yet to be.

REMEMBERING THE JOURNEY

My black Mustang convertible's top is down as I drive the Cross Island Parkway to my psychotherapy office on the south shore. The heat of the sun hasn't warmed up the day yet, but no doubt will get a lot warmer as the hours pass. Driving at this time of year, and feeling the openness of the car and the wind blowing through my hair gives me a sense of freedom mixed with a nagging sadness and nostalgia at summer being over. I'm terrible at endings of any kind. Even changes in seasons get me down. Especially fall, knowing the coldness of winter isn't far behind.

"Stop thinking so much and just enjoy the day," my mind quickly interjects, before a funk can take over.

Keeping my eyes on the road, my hand reaches down and pushes the preprogrammed button for "light radio."

I can't believe it! An old favorite from the forties is playing, and me thinking about the old days. What a welcome coincidence!

"I'll be seeing you, in all the old, familiar places. . . ." I sing along, pleased that I know almost all the words. ". . . in every lovely summer's day, I'll always think of you that way. . . . I'll find you in the morning sun. . . ."

My mind begins to wander and tune out the song still playing. It's not unusual for me to go on automatic pilot when I drive, and for thoughts and feelings to suddenly take over.

Where did all those years and people go? My longing for the past and for all those people long gone who were so close to me begins to return.

"Hold it. I'm still here." A voice speaks to me.

"Geula!" I say out loud. "I was just thinking about you."

"Well, I promised I'd never leave you. And I haven't. Right?"

"Right," I say, still shocked by her appearance. Her gentle, smiling face and piercing blue eyes flash into my mind so graphically, it's as if she's really right here in the car with me. Even her lavender scent is filling the air.

And it was true about the promise she made to never leave me. For over forty years, her words had been guiding me since the last day I was physically in her presence. Sometimes she would pop up when she knew I really needed her special guidance; at other times, she would appear because there were things that she wanted me to tell others.

But most of the time through the years, I felt only her essence around me, or heard her voice speaking inside me, although there were certain circumstances when I could actually see her. But never once had she come to me as clearly as right now. And, knowing Geula, this was no accident. There had to be a very good reason for her to be here. "Ask!" I tell myself, "or you can wait and hope she tells you, but with Geula you never know." I opt for the asking, since patience isn't one of my virtues.

"So, Geula, what's up? Why the visit today?" My words are carried away by the wind. I wait for her reply. Nothing.

Suddenly, out of nowhere, a car swerves in front of me, cutting me off to get to the exit. My heart's palpitating as I jam on the brakes to let him go. "Jerk! What's your hurry?" Nothing like fear to take my mind quickly off automatic pilot and put it back onto my driving.

I glance off to my right to get my bearings, and notice the bright yellow goldenrod growing along the shoulder of the road, strewn with black chunks of steel-belted radial tires and dented hubcaps. That's the dichotomy of living in New York—the beautiful mixed with the dirty and ugly. I know it's always there, but today it's really in my face with the car top down.

"Remember? It was an August day, just like this one, when you and I first met." Geula's voice fills my mind again.

She's back. With my eyes carefully watching the road, I turn the rest of me inward to receive all of her more clearly.

"How could I forget?" I answer aloud. "But Geula, you've never come to me this vividly before, and knowing you, it's obvious it's not just to talk about the old times. So what's up? Why are you here? There's got to be a very good reason."

"You're right." Geula answers, smiling mischievously at my catching her. "But I can't tell you yet. Just trust. You'll know when the time is right. I promise, and it'll be sooner than you think."

"Just trust, blind faith." How many times over the years had she said that?

Geula had said these words, "and you'll know when the time is right," practically from our very first meeting, and over the years I've come to understand and live by them. But today, I'm not in the mood to wait for the right time. My curiosity is piqued and I've got to know *now*.

Never having lost my childhood nosiness, I persist. "Geula, come on, why can't you tell me now?"

Her image begins to fade. "Just enjoy the beautiful day."

"Geula! Wait!" But she's gone.

I play back what's just happened and her words, over and over in my mind, trying to figure it all out. Finally, after getting absolutely nowhere, I give up.

"All right, Geula, you win. I'll let you call the shots for now and settle for the lovely weather."

As I look around at the horse chestnut trees on the bank of the road sporting a few yellow leaves, I realize it's exactly the same time of year and the same kind of day when I first "found" Geula back in 1944.

My family and I had just moved from the East Bronx to Douglaston. Actually, it was more like we fled there. My father, who normally walked around in a state of high anxiety, was even more panicked than usual by his obsession that the Nazis were going to bomb New York City, especially the boroughs of the Bronx and Brooklyn, since that's where most of the Jews lived.

In fact, the day we went house-hunting in Douglaston, he pointed excitedly to the houses as we drove up and down the tree-lined streets. "Look at the windows. See? There are no blackout shades. That means that the Germans have no intention of bombing Douglaston. We'll be safe here."

He bought our house the same day, totally convinced we would be out of danger in the event of a Nazi attack and within a very short time, I was packed up and moved away from my beloved childhood Bronx home and the most important person in my life, my Grandma Esther.

Even though Douglaston was only half an hour from the Bronx by car, they were worlds apart. On my block in the Bronx, there were old three-story attached brownstone homes and newer six-story apartment buildings. And there was always a lot of activity, beginning early in the morning and continuing throughout the day. Neighborhood women came out each afternoon to sit on their stoops and gossip while a variety of peddlers made their daily deliveries.

Douglaston, on the other hand, was a quiet half-country, half-suburban town with a mix of Tudor stuccos, like ours, center-hall colonial bricks, and one-story clapboards. Interspersed between these private homes were vacant lots on which the neighbors had staked out their "victory gardens." Growing our own vegetables to supplement our ration books, saving leftover cooking fat in empty Crisco cans, and peeling tinfoil off used cigarette packs were the patriotic things to do during World War II. My family, I was proud to say, was no exception to aiding the war effort.

And although I was able to safely walk around the neighborhood and had a freedom that I didn't have in the East Bronx, moving was devastating for me. I lost what had been my entire world, Bryant Avenue, the horse-drawn vegetable wagon, the "sweet-potato man," and the weekly trips with my grandmother to Jennings Street for the family's groceries.

"Don't put your thumb on the scale when you weigh the butter," Grandma would say as Sammy scooped a huge, pale yellow blob out of a big wooden tub and plopped it onto a piece of white waxed paper. Then she would take two dimes out of her worn, black cotton change-purse and drop them into Sammy's greasy, outstretched palm. He would nod and grin as we left the store.

Our last stop was my favorite, Jake's Pickles, situated in the alley entrance between the chicken market and the hardware store.

"Point out the pickle you want," Jake would say, looking straight at me with a dour expression on his face. And since I wanted my money's worth, I would carefully choose the biggest, fattest pickle.

"If Jake doesn't like you," Grandma would warn, "he won't sell to you." So I would point to the pickle I wanted and give Jake my biggest fake smile and my nickel, as he held the green prize out to me.

With my move to Douglaston, all those wonderful experiences were gone forever.

Literally overnight, I went from city streets to country roads. My mother went from buying fresh-baked rye bread from Cushman's Bakery to settling for prepackaged white bread and boxed cakes from the Krugs truck. Every week I eagerly waited in front of my house, anticipating the arrival of the truck, since each kid received a free Peter Wheat comic with every purchase our mothers made. But after reading my one skinny six-page comic book, the excitement was over. And although I looked forward to this weekly ritual, it never really made up for the empty hole that moving from the Bronx had created in my life.

So, in order to ease my emptiness and give me something interesting to do, I investigated the neighborhood.

Ever since my father had read *The Adventures of Huckleberry Finn* to me, I developed this fascination for exploring new places. I loved imagining that there were all kinds of wild experiences out there waiting for me. All I had to do was be adventurous enough to find them.

A favorite game I invented was my own version of the story of Hansel and Gretel. Sneaking out of my house so I wouldn't have to tell my parents where I was going, I'd scoop up a pocketful of gray gravel from my driveway. Then I'd carefully drop the tiny stones one by one behind me on the tar-paved main road every few yards or so. I chose gravel because the real Hansel and Gretel were dumb enough to drop bread crumbs. And I was too smart for that. No way was I going to let any birds have a feast at my expense.

Each day, although still cautiously staying on the main road, I used my pebbles to explore farther and farther away from home, thrilled at the idea that an exciting adventure might be waiting for me if I just kept looking.

Finally, after many days of investigating and not finding a whole lot of any interest, I decided to search out new, undiscovered territory. Leaving the now familiar road, I hiked into a huge overgrown field filled with tall grasses and a mix of all kinds of wildflowers. Trudging my way through the white Queen Anne's Lace, Black-Eyed Susans, and goldenrod, I stopped only to conduct the experiment of breaking open a milkweed pod so the creamy, sticky milk could leak out into my hands, gluing my fingers together.

Satisfied, I wiped my hands on my shorts, glanced back at the road in the distance to make sure I still had my bearings, and moved farther away and deeper into the jumble of flowers.

The sunny field melted into a dark forest that was so dense with overgrowth that the trees touched at the top, creating a green canopy overhead. I looked up at the sky, but could only see glimpses of thin rays of sunlight filtering through the leafy, entangled branches. Masses of fiddlehead ferns grew at the base of the tall oaks and pines, intermingled with wild, thorny bramble bushes that were covered with hundreds of white, red, and dark purple blackberries. Carefully, I reached my hands in between the branches, pulled off a few of the blackest berries, and popped them into my mouth. My face puckered at the sweet-sour taste, and my hands were stained purple from picking the ripe, juicy fruit. But lucky for me, a bubbling brook ran right through the middle of my newly discovered territory. As I bent down to wash my hands, the musty odor of the damp forest floor filled my nostrils. I inhaled deeply, wanting to take everything in. This place felt and smelled wonderful.

And it was all mine.

The crystal water and gurgling of the icy cold brook seemed so inviting that I sat down on the soft, mossy green bank, took off my Keds, and gingerly stepped in. My feet tingled and instantly numbed as the freezing water rushed over them.

Even though there were tiny gray fish darting around the plants growing on the sandy bottom, the water seemed clean enough to drink, so I bent over, scooped up a handful, and sampled it. Delicious! Never had I tasted water this wonderful before.

I hadn't felt so happy and satisfied since my days in the Bronx. If my father's fear of the Nazis' bombing New York came true, I could easily run for safety and hide out here. I would make a place to live underneath the bushes with an old blanket from home, eat the blackberries, and drink the fresh water from the brook. I'd more than just survive here.

Swishing my feet back and forth in the current, I pondered what made me leave the road and opt to explore this particular field today. It could have been just my curiosity, because I was desperate for any kind of new adventure. But somehow, it felt more like something was pulling me to come here. Almost like I had no choice but to follow this powerful urge inside.

Anyway, what difference did it make? It didn't really matter how or why I got here. The only thing that mattered was that from now on this special place was going to be my secret home away from home. And no one was ever going to find out about it and ruin it for me.

Satisfied with my decision, I pulled my almost-frozen feet out of the water, slipped into my sneakers, stood up, and looked around. If this was going to be my new home, then I needed to check it out further and find out exactly what was here for my use.

Where should I start? I could cross the brook and see what was on the other side or find out what was beyond the maze of blackberry bushes.

"Eenie, meenie, minie, mo," I said out loud, pointing back and forth between my two choices. Suddenly, that powerful something inside again pushed me along the bank of the brook and onto a narrow, winding dirt path. I felt helpless, yet excited, by this strange force. I had no idea where I would end up, but kept going. If this was what being possessed felt like, it was fun.

The path ended abruptly in a backyard with a tidy mowed lawn surrounded by carefully planted flowerbeds. And beyond the yard was a tan stucco and brown wood-trimmed house, a lot like mine but much larger. This wasn't supposed to happen. How could civilization be so close to my wild, uninhabited secret place? I was horrified and shocked by my discovery, but even more by an unfamiliar, middle-aged woman staring down at me.

She was taller than my father, maybe 5'9", and somehow seemed different from any woman I had ever seen before. She had a soft body, sort of straight up and down with not much of a waist, and full breasts that filled out the top of her light-blue shirtwaist dress that was buttoned all the way down the front, almost to her ankles. And peeking out from beneath the hem were nude-colored stockings and clunky black leather shoes, laced up the front with tiny perforations all over the top. The Bronx women I knew wore only high heels, even when they cleaned.

I looked up. Her salt-and-pepper gray hair was pulled straight back and tightly rolled up into a bun at the nape of her neck. A spidery hairnet kept it neatly in place. She wore no makeup on her pale, slightly wrinkled, gentle face.

And then I noticed her eyes. There was something about them. They were friendly and calm, but at the same time intense, almost piercing. It seemed as if she was looking right into me and knew exactly what I was thinking and feeling. Part of me wanted to get out of there, yet something wouldn't let me leave. I stood there frozen, unable to move.

"Hi! You've come to play with Mariel," she said, smiling down at me. "I'm her mother, Geula Franklin. We've been expecting you, Ivy." Her voice was soft and pleasant, although there was a certainty to it. I stared at her in shock, not knowing what to say.

She was expecting me? How could she possibly know I would come to her house? We had never met before, yet she sounded so sure. And scarier still, she even knew my name.

My parents' warning suddenly flashed into my mind: "Never talk to strangers." And yet, here was this woman I didn't even know who certainly was strange, saying that she was expecting me, and something inside me feeling comfortable for some unknown reason, wanting to answer her. Oddly, she seemed safe, special somehow, in a way that I couldn't quite put my finger on, but just knew. I cautiously moved toward her a few steps and began to explain, pointing behind me.

"I followed this path in the woods, back there. . . ."

Geula listened patiently, nodding and smiling at me while I awkwardly poured out my whole story.

"Well, Mariel and I are just delighted that you finally arrived," she said when I had finished. "You were sent here, so we knew you'd come. We've been waiting for you all morning."

My stomach did a somersault. Now what was she talking about? Who sent me? My mother didn't even know where I was, and I hadn't spoken to any of my friends or neighbors today who could possibly tell her. And where was this daughter, Mariel, who I was supposed to play with?

Maybe this woman was a witch or something and if I had a brain in my head I would make up some excuse while I still had the chance to get away. But before I could think of anything to say, the back door to the house flew open, and a little girl ran over to where we were standing.

"She's here! You were right, Mommy. She did come to play, just like you said."

Mariel stood grinning at me. She seemed to be about my age, with stringy blond hair that almost reached to her waist. Like a doll's. And a black patch covered her right eye. The elastic went around her head, and for a moment I thought of the pirates in the Saturday afternoon matinees my father took me to sometimes. I had never been this close to a real person who wore an eye patch.

It was too late to leave, and besides, this woman seemed harmless. Now I had lots of questions that definitely needed some answers. Like how come she wore an eye patch? And who told them I would be there? But before I could say anything, Mariel began talking excitedly.

"Do you like comic books? I get a whole bunch each month— Superman, Looney Tunes. All different kinds. Do you want to see them?"

"Yeah," I answered, forgetting about my questions. "I love reading comic books. I have Classic Comics at home. My father buys them for me, but not any of the others. What other kinds do you have? Do you have Archie? That's my most favorite."

"I have a bunch of old Archies, even the newest one. You want to read it?"

I nodded, enticed by this comic goldmine. Mariel seemed to be a normal girl, although I still wasn't so sure about her mother. Maybe while we were reading the comics together, I could nonchalantly slip in my questions, like how come they were so positive I would show up?

Mariel turned and ran toward a screened-in porch that was attached to the side of the house. I hesitated, deciding whether to follow or not. Should I go or get out of there while I still had time?

"Well, are you coming or not?" she yelled over her shoulder. Suddenly inside, something made the choice for me. There was no turning back now. "I'm coming," I called out, and dashed after her.

Mariel pulled open the porch door, plopped herself down on a faded green-cushioned glider swing, scooped a handful of comics off the floor in front of her, and began sorting through them to find the Archies.

I sat down next to her and waited, while she dropped each Archie comic she found in my lap. My eyes widened as the pile grew.

"There, that should hold you for a while," she said after she had gone through all of them. I couldn't believe how many she had.

Without a word, I took the first one off the top of the stack in my lap and began turning the cartoon-filled pages like a starved person getting her first meal in a long time. I was so engrossed in what was happening with Archie, Veronica, and Betty that I totally forgot about Mariel sitting there, watching me. And frankly, I didn't much care.

But at last, my guilt got the better of me and with great reluctance I looked up.

"Thanks, Mariel. These are great." I was sincere in my thanks, but I also wanted to make sure that she would invite me back, as I eyed the huge unread collection that I couldn't wait to get my hands on.

Now seemed as good a time as any to begin my questioning, so I reached down casually, picked up a Superman comic that was lying on the floor by my foot, and started to thumb through the pages.

"So, why do you wear that patch over your eye?" I asked, keeping my face down in the comic so I wouldn't appear too nosy.

Mariel didn't seem to be upset at all by my question. She answered as if it was nothing special. "Oh, it's because my left eye is a little weak. The patch over my right eye will make my left one work harder. The doctor called it a 'lazy eye,' but my mother says all my eye needs is loving guidance. If I speak to it and send it healthy messages, it will get stronger."

Was she kidding me? I looked up at Mariel. Her face was serious as she spoke about her eye and her mother.

"I can see you think my mother's crazy, but she's not."

"I didn't mean anything, Mariel."

"That's okay. My mother's just different than other people. She knows things. And when you get to understand her better, you'll see that what she says will happen, does."

Mariel paused, and then casually continued as if we were talking about the weather. "You know, I was adopted. My real parents were killed in a car accident, so my mother and father drove down to Virginia and brought me back to New York to be their child.

"My mother told me that she knew I belonged to her, even before I was born. She said she didn't know how or under what circumstances it would happen, but she believed it was just a matter of trusting that when the time was right, we would be together."

"I'm sorry your real parents were killed, Mariel." I was uncomfortable with her loss, but even more disturbed by the easygoing way she talked about it and accepted her mother's incredible abilities.

"Mariel, how can you be so sure that what your mother says will happen, does, and how did she know that I would come here today? My mother says a lot of things, but most of the time what she says never happens."

Mariel smiled. "When you get to spend more time with my mother, you'll see for yourself that she has special ways and knows things other people don't. It's hard to explain. Like she always says,

'You'll know when the time is right.' Kind of like today. She said the time was right for you to meet us. And you did."

Mariel slipped off the swing onto the dark-gray-painted concrete floor and began stacking the scattered comics. "I'm really glad you came to play today. Please come back again tomorrow," she said, standing up. "I have to go now and do my exercises."

"What exercises?" I asked, curious all over again. But no sooner had the word "exercises" come out of my mouth, than Geula appeared in the doorway that connected the inside of the house to the porch, as if by some invisible signal. Mariel walked over to her mother, who lovingly placed her hand on her daughter's shoulder. Geula looked at me, still sitting on the glider, smiled, and said nothing. There was no doubt that her silent smile was an indication for me to leave.

"Thank you for inviting me to play, Mrs. Franklin. I'm really glad I met you and Mariel today," I said sweetly, making sure to secure my being invited back.

"Please, call me Geula, Ivy," she answered, then looked deeply into my eyes. "And by the way, don't worry about our wanting you to come back tomorrow. We're looking forward to it." Then she paused. "We expect you to come."

And with that, Geula and Mariel disappeared into the house, leaving me on the porch alone. Goose bumps broke out all over my body as I got up off the glider. She had just read what I was thinking without my saying one word.

My mind was swimming with all kinds of questions about what had happened today as I made my way across their backyard, retracing my steps on the little path through the woods and back onto the main road. I looked down at the tarred pavement as I slowly walked toward home.

What did Geula mean, that I had been sent there? By whom?

And how did she get to know things no one else knew? And when she said, "We expect you to come," she sounded so definite, as if I had to come back. Like there was no choice. Would I? Yes. Without a doubt. I knew it, and so did Geula. There was some strange connection between us, but I couldn't figure out what it was. It was obvious that I had met someone very special in Geula. And there was no question in my mind that somehow she was going to be important in my life. But how? And how long would I have to wait to find out?

I glanced up from the road to check my bearings and was shocked to see that, in my mental wanderings, I had almost passed my own house.

Tomorrow, I would make sure to get my answers. Well, at least some of them. . . .

And in my mind I clearly heard Geula's voice. "You will. Trust me, Ivy, you will."

Visioning and Blind Faith

Nights are always too long when you have something special to do the next day. And I had two things. First, getting back to my secret hideout. And second, the Franklin house. Not to mention, leaving early was crucial since my mother was horrible in the morning. She hated to get out of bed, so the breakfasts she cooked were really disgusting. I was forced to eat runny, soft-boiled eggs with pieces of shells in them that crunched when I chewed, and drink overheated milk with gooey skin on the top. Today, I'd save us both the pain.

Quietly I pulled on my navy shorts and matching T-shirt, tip-toed down the stairs and out onto the now-familiar tar-paved road. I quickened my pace until I came to the same field, hiked through the tall grasses and wildflowers and into the dark forest. Reaching the spot where the blackberry bushes grew, I picked a handful of plump, deep-purple ones and stuffed them into my mouth. My stomach was grumbling at home before I left, but I didn't dare open the pantry or the refrigerator for fear of waking my mother. It was much more important to make a quick getaway than to eat.

Besides, the ripe berries tasted fresh and delicious. As a bonus, I had a chance to practice my war survival skills just in case my father's prophecy about the Nazis came true.

I washed the berry stains off my fingers in the brook, took a drink from my cupped hands, and retraced my steps back onto the narrow path that would lead me into the Franklins' backyard.

Once in their yard, I made my way over the lawn toward the screened-in porch where only yesterday Mariel and I had read her array of comics. Quietly I opened the screen door and stood in front of the brown paint-encrusted, wood-and-glass French doors that separated the porch from the main house. I peeked through the thin white lace curtains that covered the little windows on the inside of the door to see if Geula or Mariel were home. Also to check out what their furniture looked like. But no one seemed to be moving around inside.

Suddenly, I heard Geula's voice coming from somewhere in the house. "Your new friend's here again, Mariel."

Geula appeared from out of nowhere, opened the door, and motioned me in. "Just like I knew you would," she said, smiling.

A shiver ran through me as I stepped into the room and looked up at Geula. "Hi . . .," I stammered, apprehensively.

She was doing it again. How did she know I was there?

I hadn't knocked or slammed the porch door so that she could hear me coming, and she hadn't even looked out to see if anyone was there. She just somehow knew.

"I'm so glad you came back," Geula said, looking into my eyes.

Mariel came running in from the kitchen. "Yeah, me too," she added excitedly, waving her hand for me to follow her into the living room. "Come on, Ivy, let's play." As I cautiously walked behind her my eyes took in every detail of the room.

The interior of this house didn't look anything like mine.

Actually, it looked more like a library or a church than a regular family home. The inside walls were made of the same rough tan stucco as the outside and there were no doors separating the rooms. Instead, each room was divided by dark wood, cathedraled archways that came to a point in the center of each doorway.

An oversized, rough stone-framed fireplace without a screen was built into one of the main walls, and a gigantic bookcase covered the entire opposite wall from floor to ceiling. I had never seen so many books in one place before. Not even the public library in the Bronx or Douglaston had a wall full of books like that. There was every kind of book possible. Several sets of encyclopedias, rows and rows of novels, art books, and biographies. And there must have been at least a hundred books on all sorts of other subjects, and a whole shelf of Bibles.

"Mariel," I whispered. "Who reads all these books?"

"My mother," Mariel called over her shoulder. "She likes to read a lot. She knows everything. If you want to know about anything at all, just ask her."

I slowed my pace, attempting to take in all the titles.

Mariel turned and glared at me. "Stop staring at the books and let's go upstairs to my room. You're wasting our play time." Her voice had an obvious tone of annoyance because my full attention wasn't focused on her, but I couldn't help it.

My eyes were glued to the books as I followed Mariel to the far end of the living room, where an uncarpeted, dark oak, narrow, winding stairway led us up to the second floor of the house.

"Hurry up," Mariel called out as we reached the top step. "We're almost at my room." She led me into a medium-sized bedroom with a low, slanted ceiling and two single beds. But not ordinary beds. High, dark, wooden beds, covered with burgundy-red chenille spreads. I'd never seen beds so high. The top of the mattress was almost up to my shoulders.

"Your beds are so strange. Why are they like that?"

"'Cause they're very old. My mother said they have been in her family a long, long time. This one is mine." Mariel pointed to the bed with a Victorian doll sprawled on the spread-covered pillow. "And that's my mother's bed," she said, pointing to the one next to hers.

She slept in the same room as her mother? I had never heard of anything like that before. All the parents I knew slept in the same bed together. Mine did. And I knew she had a father because she told me her parents came to Virginia to get her when her real parents died.

"Where does your father sleep? Why don't you have your own room?"

"Because I sleep in here with Mommy," she said, irritated that I didn't understand. "Daddy sleeps in the room next to us. My mother says that she has so many things to teach me that there aren't enough hours in the day. So we even talk at night before I go to sleep."

"What does your mother teach you that's so important that you have to learn even at night?"

"Oh, lots of different things."

"Like what, for instance?"

Mariel, annoyed by my persistence, swept the stuffed animals off the top of a wooden toy chest next to her bed and onto the floor. "Stop asking so many questions. You'll find out later. Now, do you want to play a game or not?"

I nodded yes, but I was a lot more interested in hearing about her mother. I wanted to know everything about this family that was so different from my own. But it was obvious I would have to wait to get my answers. Right now, Mariel had no interest in being of any help.

I reached into the toy chest. "You've got 'Authors'! My favorite game. You want to play it?" I said, attempting to placate Mariel before she decided to send me home.

"Yeah, I'm good at 'Authors.'" Her mood instantly changed and she seemed happy again as she sat down on the round, multicolored braided rug and took the deck from me. She dumped the cards out on the rug between us, then dealt us each a hand and concentrated on the ones she got.

"Do you have any Sir Walter Scotts?"

I quickly scanned my cards. "No. Do you have. . . ." But before I could finish my sentence, Geula appeared in the doorway.

"Girls, when you finish your game, we'll do our exercises. I'll wait for you down in the living room. Don't take too long."

I couldn't believe my ears. Geula had just invited me to do exercises with them! Instantly I lost interest in playing anymore and put my cards down.

"Mariel, what kinds of exercises are we going to do? Sit-ups or jumping jacks? I did those every day in school in the Bronx."

Mariel giggled.

"What's so funny?" I asked, embarrassed by her laughing at me.

"They're mind exercises, silly. You'll see. We'd better go now." Mariel became serious as she put down the cards and stood up. She headed for the staircase with me close behind, made her way into the living room where Geula told us to meet, and plopped herself down onto the huge threadbare rug in front of the bookcase. I did the same.

Mariel reached up into her hair, loosened the elastic, slid her eye patch off, and dropped it down on the rug. I turned toward her so I could get a really good look at her exposed right eye and was surprised to see that it seemed exactly the same as the other one.

"Mariel, do you really need to wear that eye patch?" I asked.

"Your eye looks normal to me. I can't see anything wrong with it. Maybe you really don't need that patch."

"No. I have to wear it. Things are blurry when I look at them, but with my mother's exercises and the patch, they're getting clearer every day."

"Mariel," I persisted, "if I do the exercises with you today, how will they help my eyes if I can see good already?"

Before she could answer me, Geula walked into the room and motioned for us to move farther apart so there would be room for her to sit between us. Instead of sitting though, as I expected, she knelt down on the rug as if she were going to pray. Mariel got onto her knees too, so I followed.

Geula turned and looked into my eyes. "These exercises will help your body by talking to your mind," she said softly.

I was about to interrupt and ask her to explain what she meant and why we were doing the exercises, but before I could say anything Geula quickly answered my unspoken questions. "One day you'll know. For now, please just join us."

From the intensity of her face, I knew to obey and fell silent.

Then she turned back and stared straight ahead of her. "Let's begin by holding hands," she said, reaching her left hand out to Mariel and her right one out to me.

"First," Geula continued, "we're going to relax by doing some deep breathing. We do that because our bodies and minds learn more when we're relaxed. So what I want you to do now is to listen and follow exactly what my words tell you to do. Okay?"

Mariel and I nodded. It was obvious from Geula's tone that she didn't expect any other answer.

Geula's voice became gentle and calm as she began the exercise.

"Take a deep breath in through your nose . . . feel the air filling out your lungs all the way up to your neck . . . hold your breath . . .

hold it. . . . Now exhale . . . and let your chest go loose completely as you breathe all the air out.

"And again . . . breathe in deeply . . . let your chest expand as fully as you can . . . hold it . . . hold it. . . . Now let your lungs empty as you breathe out . . . feel your whole body relax. . . .

"Keep on breathing in . . . and out . . . in . . . and out . . . smoothly . . . easily . . . allow the air to just flow in and out of you as your body relaxes and your mind becomes more alert and open to hearing my voice and words."

I did as Geula instructed and felt my whole body begin to go limp. Her words and the sound of her voice were so soothing and hypnotizing that I didn't mind doing what she said. This exercise felt nice, but for the life of me, I couldn't figure out how was breathing going to help Mariel's eye and my mind.

Geula's voice droned on. "Feel the relaxation flowing through you. . . and let your mind and body become receptive to healing as you listen and follow my words."

"As you continue breathing . . . close your left eye, and squeeze it tight . . . tighter . . . tighter still. Keep your eye closed and now imagine a very bright white light shining straight into your eye. This light has special powers to heal your eye, to make it healthy and your eyesight perfect.

"Let the light surround your eyeball . . . feel it shine through the surface, into the very center itself. Now repeat along with me, 'God bless my left eye,' and as you say it, know that the light is healing your eye, feel your sight becoming stronger and stronger."

I followed Geula's lead and chanted "God bless my left eye" six times, along with Mariel, and although I couldn't really tell if anything was happening, I figured it might help and definitely couldn't hurt.

Then Geula switched our attention to healing our right eyes.

We did that six times too, and then both eyes together. Each time with the same deep breathing, the bright light with the healing power, and the "God bless" chanting.

I peeked at Mariel and Geula while we were exercising, expecting to see something magical happening in the room. Maybe a ghostlike image floating around. But nothing was different.

All of a sudden, Geula stopped chanting and stared straight ahead into space as if she was somewhere else and not in the room with Mariel and me. She seemed to be looking at someone I couldn't see, some invisible spirit maybe.

I bent forward and checked out Mariel to see if she was bothered by her mother's odd behavior. Apparently not, because her eyes were also open as she smiled back at me.

I looked at Geula again, but her eyes were still unfocused, as if she was in some kind of trance. Then, without a word and without focusing on either of us, she turned toward Mariel and placed her open hands, palms down, on the top of Mariel's head. She kept them there for a few minutes, without saying a word. I knew that whatever Geula was doing to Mariel, my turn would be next. I felt nervous yet somehow safe as I waited.

Finally, Geula took her hands off Mariel's head, rubbed them together, and placed them the same way on top of my head. There was a strange tingling sensation under my scalp that flowed from her fingertips all the way down through my whole body. I hardly felt Geula's hands on me at all, yet that invisible power she told us about was amazingly strong. It felt as if a gentle electrical current had run right through me. But it didn't hurt. Instead, I felt warm and full of energy.

I couldn't wait for the exercises to be over so I could ask Mariel if there was any difference in her eye. And, if the opportunity presented itself, to get some answers from Geula. My questions for her were piling up more than ever.

"There, all done," Geula said suddenly, and stood up. "You girls can go play now. I'll leave a plate of orange slices out on the porch table for you." She walked nonchalantly toward the kitchen. She and Mariel acted as if we had just gone through some ordinary, everyday exercise routine. And maybe for them it was, but not for me.

Mariel looked over at me. "What's wrong, Ivy? You're frowning."

I didn't want to tell Mariel that I was afraid that if Geula could heal Mariel's eye and knew that I was coming two days in a row, maybe she could also read my mind and uncover this terrible secret I had been hiding from everybody, even God.

"Nothing," I answered quickly, hoping to cover my anxiety. Then I diverted the focus. "If you want, I could get the box of 'Authors' from your room and bring it out on the porch, or we could read comics. Which would you like to do?"

"Let's read!" she said, jumping to her feet, and tugging at my arm as we headed toward the porch.

Mariel reached down for an Archie comic and thumbed through it as we sat back down on the glider.

I leaned forward and stared into her face. "Mariel, can I ask you a personal question?"

Mariel returned my look. "Sure. What is it?"

"Can you see any better since we exercised? I mean, is your eye any different now? Because when your mother put her hands on my head there was something like electricity and now I feel somehow really good. It wasn't this way before we exercised."

I didn't tell her I also felt worried, but that part was only for me to know.

Mariel closed one eye and then the other, testing out her sight. "I can't really tell if there's any difference. My eyesight seems to be about the same. But I'm pretty sure it has to be improving, because my mother told me that what you say to your mind, you say to your body. And when we were all doing the exercises I kept telling my eye, 'Get better, get better,' so I know it has to be improving."

"But how can you be sure?" I persisted. This wasn't the answer I was looking for.

"I just am!" Mariel snapped back. "Don't you remember what I told you earlier about my mother? That what she says will happen, does? So stop asking."

I nodded and gave in, not totally satisfied. For the moment, I decided to go along with what Mariel was saying. Besides her face and voice told me that she was done talking.

Geula joined us on the porch, carrying a chipped white ceramic plate filled with orange sections. She placed it down on the glass-topped, wrought-iron table in front of the glider.

"Here. Eat up!" she said without looking at us and turned to walk back into the house.

"Wait, Geula," I quickly called out to stop her from leaving. "Can I ask you a question?"

She turned back and looked at me seriously. "Of course, Ivy. What is it?"

"Yesterday . . .," I began nervously, "how did you know that I was coming to play with Mariel?"

As the last word came out, my stomach knotted. Maybe I should have kept my big mouth shut, but I had to know.

I waited in silence, hoping Geula would say something to ease my mounting anxiety. Instead, she just sat there staring at me for what seemed forever. Finally she spoke.

"I was waiting for you to ask," she began with a smile. "You like to have all the answers, don't you?" And as her expression relaxed so did my stomach.

I nodded and smiled back at her. This woman was like no adult

I had ever known. She not only didn't tell me to stop asking questions and shut up, but was actually *encouraging* me!

Geula moved toward the arm of the glider and sat down.

"Your question is a little complicated, but let's see if I can explain it simply. I just knew in here," she said, pointing to her head. Then she pointed to her chest. "And in here. I've learned to trust and believe what I call information that comes into my heart and mind.

"You look confused. Let me explain. That information that I'm talking about comes into you in the form of an urge or a thought that you weren't even thinking about, but somehow pops in. Sort of like an inside message from somewhere out there. I'm not exactly sure where it comes from. All I know is that I have to trust and follow it without question."

"Is that how you knew I was coming yesterday?" I asked.

Geula nodded. "Actually yes. Even your name was given to me. I got the information inside, and I knew without a doubt you were coming here. And since I trust my information, I was out in the backyard waiting for you."

Geula leaned forward. "And you. Why were you in the woods, and how come you followed the path you did and not another one? There were others to choose from, weren't there?"

"Yeah, but this one just seemed to be the only one to take."

"Why was it the only one to take?" she continued, pressing me further.

"I don't know. It just felt like it was."

"Exactly my point!" Geula said triumphantly. "You didn't know why. But you chose it for some unknown reason that seemed right. See? There isn't a logical answer.

"There are a lot of things that happen that we don't logically understand. Things we can't find any reason for, or why they're happening to us at this particular time. That's the information I'm talking about. You just feel it and know it. Am I making myself clear?"

I nodded. "Yeah, completely."

Geula smiled and looked pleased. "You see, most of our experiences don't make much sense when we try to figure them out logically, but they do when we accept and trust the information we get. Another name for it is 'blind faith.' In fact, we can actually enjoy playing with this blind faith as a kind of an adventure game."

"How?" I quickly interjected, liking games of all sorts, especially adventure ones.

"All you have to do," Geula continued, "is trust everything that is happening to you and around you, and believe that whatever is taking place is happening exactly the way it's supposed to, and exactly at the right time."

I sat looking at Geula, taking in what she had just said, but something wasn't sitting right with me.

"Geula," I began disagreeing. "I can't go along with trusting and believing in everything. It's okay for the good things, but how can I trust and believe that bad things are supposed to happen?"

Geula answered quickly. "You must. I mean everything. Even the frustrating and unhappy times. Every situation comes into your life for you to learn from and grow. Remember what I said, everything that happens, happens for a good reason. You just won't always understand or know why."

Geula put her hand on my shoulder and smiled reassuringly.

"So now that you understand, let me ask you a question. Do you think when you play this blind faith game you can try to take every day as it comes and trust that you need everything that happens to you?"

I nodded. "I'll try," I said, "But it won't be easy accepting the bad things."

Geula shook her head in agreement, then said solemnly, "I know. But you must. Okay?"

"Okay," I answered obediently, suddenly knowing that what she had said was important.

"Good. And I promise, you will get all your answers when the time is right." Geula patted my arm, then stood up and smoothed the back of her dress.

"Those oranges look very tasty." She reached over, took one, and popped it into her mouth. "Mmmm good" I heard her say as she disappeared back into the kitchen.

Mariel reached over, took an orange section and bit into it. From her expression it was obvious that she had no interest in my conversation with her mother, and was glad it was over so we could get back to something really important, like playing.

I reached for a piece of orange too, but held it in my hand as I continued thinking about all Geula had said.

I kind of liked the idea of not thinking so much and taking each situation as it came, and believing that one day it would make good sense. It seemed kind of a welcome relief from all the worrying I was used to doing over things I couldn't control or figure out.

Mariel pulled the orange rind out of her mouth and dropped it onto the plate.

"You want to play library instead of reading?" she asked, juice dribbling down her chin. "I can get the date stamper from my father's desk."

"You've got an ink pad too?" I asked and handed a paper napkin to her. And immediately wondered what lesson or information I was going to get from playing library and eating oranges.

"Blind faith, remember? Stop trying to figure it out." Geula's voice popped into my mind. "You'll know when the time is right."

"Will you stop daydreaming?" Mariel's irritated voice shook me out of my thoughts.

"Are we going to play library, or are you going to sit there all day staring into space?"

"Sorry, Mariel. I'm ready now," I said sheepishly, and followed her into the house toward the staircase.

EXPERIMENTS

Something odd caught my eye as I walked up the stairs after Mariel to get the date stamper. She kept on going, but that "something" forced me to stop and turn back. There was an assortment of peculiar objects inside Geula's mahogany curio cabinet, which stood next to the bottom of the landing. I had walked up and down the stairs before, but hadn't paid much attention to the cabinet or noticed the contents on the glass shelves. Probably because I expected that Geula's cabinet would have a collection of miniature china cups and saucers and various heirlooms from dead relatives like my mother and grandmother kept in theirs. But with Geula, I should have known better. With her, anything was possible. The weirder the better.

I knelt down to get a better look at the objects on each of the three glass shelves in the cabinet. On every single shelf there were rocks of many shapes and sizes and colors. Rocks! Nothing else was in the cabinet, just rocks. One was rust-colored and shaped like a heart. Another was dark brown with a white checkmark in the center, not painted on, but actually in the rock itself.

I practically had to lay down on my side and press my nose to the glass to get a good look at the oddest rock of all on the bottom shelf. It was bright orange with a wrinkled surface that looked exactly like a big chunk of dried-out orange peel. That one was the best.

Why would Geula be displaying rocks in a cabinet where most people kept their important treasures, I pondered. Whether she liked it or not, this question had to be asked now. I wasn't going to wait for some future information. That would take too long.

"Mariel," I called out, before she could wonder what happened to me and maybe get annoyed again. "Start taking the books out, I'll be with you in a minute." Truthfully, at this point I had lost interest in playing library or anything else for that matter, except for getting information about those rocks.

I moved even closer for a better look at my favorite one, the orange rock. If only I could feel the wrinkles.

"Lovely, isn't it?" Geula said, kneeling down next to me.

I jumped, startled by her being there.

"I saw you stop and do a double-take from the kitchen," Geula said, pointing to the orange one. "Isn't this rock amazing? What do you think of it?"

"Unbelievable," I answered, still looking at the wrinkled rock. I had never seen anything like this before. Ever. Anywhere. "It looks like a piece of petrified orange skin. Each one of your rocks is so interesting. Where did you find them all, and why do you keep them in your cabinet? No grown-up I know collects rocks, and for sure they would never leave them out for people to see. They'd be too embarrassed. Only kids do stuff like this."

Geula smiled, keeping her eyes on the rocks in the cabinet. "That's why I admire children. They know more about what's valuable and important than most adults I know.

"Do you collect anything?" she asked.

"Yeah, I've saved some great things," I boasted, trying to catch Geula's eye. "Last summer I found the most beautiful white seagull feather at Orchard Beach, when my father and I went fishing. It's pure white with beige on the tip. And I also discovered this weird pink and white shell that looks exactly like my Aunt Daisy's teeth and gums. I swear! I'm not kidding!"

Geula nodded, turning toward me. "I believe you. So tell me, what attracted you to the feather and the 'teeth' shell? What made you pick them up?"

That was a good question. I had never really thought about why before, except that they were interesting and I liked collecting things.

"I don't know, exactly, Geula. Something about them caught my eye. The feather was so soft and beautiful and the 'teeth' shell was so real-looking, that I just had to have them. I thought they were special. Do you know what I mean?"

"Absolutely," she said, nodding. "But did you ever wonder how come you got to find them and no one else did? They were right out in plain sight for anyone to take. Right?"

"Maybe I was lucky or maybe nobody else wanted them," I guessed.

"Or," Geula interrupted, "maybe they were there only for *you* to find, and that's why no one else picked them up or even saw them."

I shook my head. "That's impossible, Geula. They were right out there in the open on the beach."

"That's true," she agreed, "but just because something is right in front of someone, doesn't mean they're going to see it, especially if they have no feeling for it, or there's no reason for them to see it. If we're meant to find something, we do, and if we're not meant to find it, we don't. And *you* were meant to find and have that shell and that feather."

"But why was I supposed to find them?"

"Because for some important reason, you were intended to have them. Everyone is supposed to have certain things. That's why they're attracted to their own choice of objects. The ones that are only for them.

"You know, the same thing happens to me, too. That's exactly how I found each one of my special rocks," Geula said, looking at the cabinet. "I swear each one called out to me, 'Pick me up. I'm here especially for you.' Strangely, there was no way I couldn't *not* pick up each of my rocks. If I tried to walk past, thinking, 'nice but I don't need that,' something inside me here, said, 'Yes you do! Go back.'" Geula pointed to the information spot on her chest. "It was as if I didn't have a choice, and couldn't leave without obeying.

"So tell me, did it happen for you that way, too?"

"Yeah, it did," I answered, nodding. "I had this urge in my body that I can't exactly describe, that said, 'You must have it. Don't walk away.' It's too hard to explain, Geula. All I know is, I love taking out all my stuff and examining it. Over and over. And I'm going to keep every single thing. Forever."

Geula smiled. "Me too." Then she added, "You know what I think? I think the reason we're attracted to certain objects is because there's something special in them only for us."

"What do you mean?" I asked suddenly confused. "What something special could be in my feather, for instance?"

"Well, when you look at it long enough, it could bring up a memory, or maybe a thought or an idea can pop into your head. Like it did with Daedalus, for example. Ever hear about him?"

I shook my head, wondering what idea he had, whoever he was, and then waited for Geula to tell me.

"Do you know anything about Greek mythology?" she asked.

I shook my head again.

"Then let me tell you. Mythology was a type of religion that took place hundreds of years ago, and explained the world through stories of gods and legendary heroes. Daedalus, who was an architect and sculptor, was one of those heroes.

"The myth says that he did something to offend the king of Crete, and got himself and his son, Icarus, thrown in prison. One day, Daedalus saw a bird flying and it gave him an idea for an escape. He made two pairs of large wings out of feathers and wax, and fastened them to their shoulders for their getaway. And it worked, too. He and Icarus flew away, but, not listening to Daedalus' warning about the heat of the sun, Icarus flew too close to it and the wax holding the wings together melted and poor Icarus fell into the sea."

"Icarus should have listened and stayed away," I interjected, bothered by his stupidity. "But it was still a good idea anyway because it worked for his father."

Geula nodded. "You're right. However, it was more than just a good idea. It was brilliant, because centuries later, it gave the artist and inventor Leonardo da Vinci the model for his flying machine. And if you look at Leonardo's sketches of the machine, they show a man with large wings attached to his shoulders, flying.

"That's why I believe the objects we collect are more special and important than we even realize. If we allow our minds to flow freely, our objects can be an unbelievable resource to stimulate our creativity. Just look at the incredible make-believe games you and Mariel create out of empty boxes and my clothes."

My eyes lit up at the thought. "I once took old window shades and painted all kinds of scenes on them for a play," I added.

"Great idea," Geula said, smiling approvingly.

Suddenly she fell silent and stared into her cabinet.

"And you know what else I think?" Geula paused. "I think that sometimes when we need to move in a new direction or learn some-thing new, or even find answers to problems that we have to solve, we can use our creative mind the same way, only without an object.

"You know who did that?" Without waiting for my answer, she replied, "Albert Einstein! Do you know who he is?"

"Yeah," I said, "but all I know about him is that he's a scientist with wild, bushy hair and that he escaped from the Nazis."

Geula smiled. "That's right. And the creating or problem solv-ing that he did in his mind without an object, he called 'thought experiments.'

"As a scientist, he was working on some of his new theories about space and time, and because he couldn't do experiments in a laboratory to test out his ideas, he tested them by taking long walks in the country and thinking in mental pictures. Then, after he saw the pictures, he took all the information he got, and creat-ed new, never before thought of, scientific knowledge. What do you think of that?"

"Geula, that's incredible," I said, nodding in amazement. "But Einstein's a brilliant scientist. Ordinary people can't do what he did. No way."

"Oh, yes they can," she interrupted. "Anyone can do it if they try. And they don't have to be brilliant or a scientist."

She leaned forward. "Why don't you try it? See if you can get information by taking one of your real objects or just by using nothing but an idea of yours, like Einstein did in his 'thought experiment.'"

"But Geula . . .," I then said defensively, "it's going to be too hard."

"Never mind 'but,'" she answered with an edge to her voice. "Give it a try. You have a great imagination. Use it and see what comes into your mind."

"Okay, but how?" I felt like I was on the spot. "I don't even know how to start."

"Let me help you. It's really not that difficult." Geula's voice softened. "Take your feather, for example. All you have to do is look at it for a minute or hold it, and then think about what it means to you. Then just close your eyes and wait. Let your imagination run wild with any pictures, scenes, or thoughts that pop up. Accept it all and don't censor anything, no matter how crazy it seems. Then open your eyes and think about whatever came into your mind and how you could possibly use this information for new ideas. And after that, use that blind faith we talked about, and try putting some of your good ideas into action. It's that simple. That's what Einstein did. And who knows? With your good mind, I'll bet you'll discover talents and abilities we don't even know about yet."

I grinned, feeling my face turn red in embarrassment and pride.

Geula smiled back and then turned her eyes toward the contents of the cabinet.

"Do you know why I keep every one of these rocks in here?"

I shook my head.

"To honor them all for the ideas they gave me. And because of their gifts to me, each one is more valuable than a jewel."

Geula stopped speaking, turned to face me, and looked directly into my eyes. Her expression became more serious than I had ever seen before. It was obvious there was a very important reason in her mind, but from her look, I knew better than to ask why. Besides, I could tell whatever it was, was big by the way the hair stood up on my arm. That only happened when things were very special or something unusual was going to happen in the future.

"Honey," she began again, "tonight when you're at home, take something out of your collection, anything that especially seems to call to you. Then close your eyes, and see what pictures pop into your imagination. Or maybe when you walk home from here later, try a 'thought experiment' and see what idea or information comes up. From now on, I want you to make it a daily habit to become more aware of whatever comes into your mind. Take it very seriously and don't discount or forget anything that happens. Store everything in your memory. After all, who knows when things will come together for good use down the road?

"Will you do that for me?"

I nodded. There was no doubt from the tone of her voice that she was telling me, not asking. And inside my mind I heard loud and clear, "This will be good for you. Do what she says."

Then her face softened and she changed back into an ordinary mother again.

"By the way," she said lightly, "Mariel's been awfully quiet."

"Maybe she fell asleep waiting for me." I felt guilty for staying away from Mariel so long, but I was glad for any contact with Geula. And oh, how I wished with all my heart at that moment, that she could be my mother.

Geula laughed. "No. If I know Mariel, she probably heard me talking about the rocks and decided to play instead. I don't blame her. She's heard about them too many times."

"Go have fun, library is a great game," Geula said casually as she walked toward the kitchen.

I was startled. Mariel and I hadn't said anything about playing library when Geula was in the room. How did she know what we were going to do?

I climbed the stairs slowly.

Without question, I would try the "object experiment" later in my room, probably with my feather, but definitely not when either of my parents might walk in on me. How would I possibly be able to explain what I was doing or tell them about Geula? And for sure, they wouldn't appreciate or understand the "God bless" exercises and the way she was healing Mariel's eye. They would probably think Geula was nuts, and not allow me to go to that amazing house again. I had to protect us both. There was nobody like Geula. And no way could she or Mariel try to convince me that she was just an ordinary mother. I knew deep in my heart that she was someone special. And just like the rocks she collected, somehow she had selected me. And that my finding her was definitely no accident either.

Maybe one day I would know who she was, besides just Mariel's mother. I patted my chest.

Of that I was very, very sure.

RECEIVERS OF INFORMATION

The glare of the morning sun made my eyes water and I had to squint as I ran through the field and into the shade of the forest toward the brook. I pulled off my sneakers and stepped into the icy cold water. Ahhh . . . What a relief! The back of my neck was covered in sweat and it felt wonderful to be cooling off at last.

Swishing my feet around in the gentle current, I reached down to grab the half-full box of saltine crackers that I had cleverly snuck out of the house, and began munching one. Smart that I thought to hide them in my room last night for my early morning getaway. I took another bite, enjoying the salty taste. Good thing someone invented crackers, or I'd starve to death. Crackers were the only thing I could safely take to eat without getting into trouble, since all the food in our house was earmarked for something, even leftovers. Everything was either for lunch, dinner, or my father. So from the time I was little, I learned to eat saltines whenever I was hungry.

And this morning they would go very nicely along with the fresh water, as a tasty and filling breakfast.

I could feel the perspiration trickle down my back as I chewed a mouthful of dry crackers. Too bad that I had left so fast and hadn't thought to put on my bathing suit. Dunking my feet felt great, but it would have been even better to splash around in the cold water or sit in it up to my neck. Of course the best of all would be swimming in a pool or at the Douglaston beach. But that was definitely out of the question for me forever.

My father never let me go to any public pools or wade at the Douglaston beach, much less swim there. And my asking him would only get me a big NO! and one of his lectures.

"Do you know why pools are warm?" he would begin. "Because people pee in them! Do you want to swim in that kind of water?" the lecture went on and on.

He never made any sense to me because I saw lots of people swimming in Starlight Pool when we drove by it on our way to the Bronx to visit on Sunday. I was dying to ask him that if the pool was so disgusting, how come it was packed with people swimming and laughing and having a good time? I wanted to hear him explain that one. But I knew better than to start up with my father. He could be impossible when he didn't get his way. Instead I silently watched, angry at him and jealous of the happy swimmers.

And forget about his lecture on the dangers of the Douglaston beach. That one was a beauty.

"Swim at that filthy beach? Are you crazy? All of New York City's sewers empty into that water. But, go ahead, be a smart aleck, swim there. You'll end up like Timmy Reilly with polio. Spend your life in an iron lung, if going to the beach is that important to you."

There was absolutely no point in trying to reason with him. He would just work on convincing me even more that *he* was right and that I didn't know what I was talking about.

Every time he wore me down, and I gave in, but I never believed one word he said.

In spite of his constant worrying and ridiculous limits on me, I found lots of ways to make myself happy. Like wading in this refreshing brook, for instance, which he didn't know about and never would, if I could help it. I didn't like lying, but what choice did he give me?

Well, he couldn't control my mind, and in there I was free to go to the Douglaston beach as many times as I liked.

I closed my eyes the way Geula taught me to do using Einstein's "thought experiment" and imagined myself playing in the sand and splashing in the water at the Douglaston beach, when suddenly, Mariel and Geula were there in the picture with me. Mariel was playing in the water, and Geula was sitting on a navy blue beach blanket. I even saw a green thermos jug next to her. Either I had the best, most powerful imagination, or it was my longing and wishful thinking.

I opened my eyes and looked at my watch. Almost ten o'clock. Perfect! Definitely not too early to visit Geula and Mariel. Even my mother would be getting out of bed by now. I pushed my wet feet into my sneakers, picked up my box of crackers, and made my way along the path into the Franklins' backyard.

Mariel saw me coming and waved from the porch.

"Hi. Come on over. I'm eating toast with quince jelly. My mother made it. You want some?"

"Yeah," I called back, pulling open the porch door. I slid onto the glider next to Mariel and put the box of crackers down on the glass-topped table. "Do you think the jelly would taste good on crackers too? I brought some from home. And what's quince jelly, anyhow? I never even heard of a quince."

"It's a fruit, sort of like a little apple. I picked them from the quince tree in the yard over there," Mariel said, pointing to the side of her house. "And my mother cooked them into jelly. Here, it's good. Have a taste."

I took the piece of toast that she held out to me and bit into it. "You're right," I said, swallowing a mouthful. "This jelly's delicious. Thanks."

"I just came from dunking my feet in the brook to cool off. Today's going to be a scorcher, so do you want to go back there and wade after we finish eating?"

"No, let's stay here," Mariel quickly replied, "because my mother said it's going to get even hotter later, and when the tide gets high enough, she's going to take us swimming at the Douglaston beach."

At her words my body broke out into goose pimples and it couldn't be because I was cold. Not in this ridiculous heat.

I looked at her in shock, then answered, "Mariel, I can't believe what you just said. That's the weirdest. Before, when I was sitting at the brook, I imagined that I was swimming at the Douglaston beach and you and your mother were in the picture. But that was only my wishful thinking. We can't really go there because my father said the beach water was polluted and that I'd get polio if I swim there.

"I know your mother would never let you do anything that was dangerous, so how come she lets you swim there? My next-door-neighbor, Timmy Reilly, swam there last summer and now his leg is crippled because he got polio from the dirty water."

Mariel seemed shaken up. "That can't be true! My mother has taken me there lots of times to swim. She would never take me to the beach if I could get sick from the water. Although . . . she does check it out first."

"What do you mean, 'check it out'? How?"

"With God," Mariel replied. "She asks God if it's clean. And if the answer is yes, she takes me swimming."

Her comment jolted me. "You're kidding. Right?"

"No, I'm not. I swear."

"Does God really talk to her?" I pressed further, not believing my ears. "Did you ever hear his voice?"

"No. But, it's not like the way we're talking now, it's more like when we do the 'God bless' exercises. She hears the answer inside herself and then she knows what to do. So if the water's okay, do you want to go or not?"

Loud and clear, I could hear my father's warning in my head, but my gut feeling and my sweating body said, "Do it!" without a moment's hesitation.

"Yeah, I'll go," I answered quickly, "but I forgot to wear a bathing suit today, of all days."

"Don't worry about it, I've got an extra one you can use. Let's go find my mother and ask her if the water's clean. Okay?"

Mariel didn't wait for me to answer. She excitedly ran into the kitchen where Geula was standing over the sink, washing the breakfast dishes.

"Mommy, did God say the water's clean today?" she began babbling rapidly. "You said if it was, we could go swimming. Can we go? Should I get my bathing suit on?"

Geula smiled at Mariel. "Whoa there! Hold your horses. Give me a minute, and I'll check it out for you." Then she turned her attention toward me. "Good morning, Ivy. I'm glad you're here to join us."

"Me, too!" I answered, returning her smile. "Can we really go swimming at the beach?"

"We'll see. I'm going to find out right now."

Geula put down the cup she was washing, wiped her hands on her apron, and faced the open window over the sink that looked out into her backyard.

I watched every move Geula made. I didn't want to miss a single detail on how she was going to get this information from God.

She took several deep breaths, just like she did with the "God bless" exercises and closed her eyes. I moved closer to her and strained to hear some voice, Geula's or God's, but all I heard was the sound of Geula's deep breathing in the quiet of the room. I kept my eyes on her face for some clue as to what might be going on inside of her, but she just looked like she was peacefully sleeping while standing up.

I looked over at Mariel, who returned my look by rolling her eyes toward the ceiling with an impatient expression on her face and a shrug of her shoulders.

It felt like an hour that we were waiting for our answer, but it couldn't have been more than a couple of minutes before Geula finally opened her eyes and turned around to face us.

"I got the okay," she said, satisfied. "The water will be wonderful for swimming today, girls. Mariel, put on your blue two-piece bathing suit and take the two old striped bath towels out of the linen closet. High tide will be at noon, so hurry, and get ready." Then as if nothing odd had just happened, Geula went back to washing the dishes. Mariel matter-of-factly ran upstairs to put on her bathing suit and get the towels. I just stood there dumbfounded. Maybe Mariel was used to her mother talking to God, or maybe she thought everyone's mother did. But, I could assure her, Geula was like no one I had ever known. Not my parents or any of my relatives. Nobody.

Geula glanced over her shoulder. "Why are you standing there? What's wrong? Don't you want to put on a bathing suit?"

I hesitated for a moment. "I will, but first Geula, can I ask you something?"

"Sure, what is it?"

"Before when you said you would find out if we could go to the beach, how did you get the answer? Did you talk to someone . . .,"

I stammered, "like God? Mariel said you ask God."

Geula put down the dish she was holding, and turned to look at me. She stared into my eyes without speaking for what seemed to be a very long time. Her serious expression and the deadly silence brought back the old familiar knot in my stomach that had a way of totally paralyzing my whole body and mind. Maybe she was mad at me for asking such a personal question. After all, my father used long silences when he was angry with me. Sometimes he would be silent for days. Then, when he finally talked again, he would sternly lecture me. "Think before you talk because once it's out of your mouth, you can't take it back" and "It's better to be safe than sorry." And his deadly silent treatment proved him right.

Geula remained silent as she pulled out one of the chrome tubular kitchen chairs and motioned for me to sit down. Then she seated herself in the one opposite.

Here it comes, I thought, and held my breath, ready for the big lecture on my nosy behavior, but instead Geula's voice was soft as she began speaking.

"That's an excellent question, and I'm so pleased that you asked it," she said, smiling.

I was shocked. A compliment instead of a criticism? I couldn't believe it. This behavior was almost as peculiar as Geula's talking to God. But who cared?

Geula leaned forward in her chair to get as close to me as possible.

"It's really easy to get answers," she began. "Even from God. Would you like to know how to do it?"

"Yeah, very much. How do I start?" I said excitedly.

She seemed pleased by my response. "Let's see if I can explain this simply.

"When your body relaxes like it does in our exercises and then you close your eyes, your mind is able to shut off everything on the outside around you. And when your mind is blank, it's much more powerful and able to open up to information and pictures that you couldn't get otherwise. You can see things and know things inside yourself that you would never know if your eyes were open and busy taking in everything that's going on around you.

"So to get my answer about the beach I closed my eyes, took a few deep breaths to relax my body and clear my mind, and then when my mind was totally blank, I internally asked the question, 'Is the water clean today for swimming?' And then I waited until a picture came onto my empty mental screen. It was of you and Mariel and a lot of other people playing and swimming in the water at the Douglaston beach. At the same time I saw the image of the beach, I had this very definite feeling all over my body that the water was safe for swimming. But then to be extra sure, I waited for the deciding answer. Finally, inside of me, I heard the word 'yes.'"

"Geula, was that God?"

"In a way, I guess," she replied thoughtfully. "God, universe . . . what name we decide to call whoever or whatever gives us the knowledge, that's what it is to us. But what really matters is that we're given the answers we need for absolutely everything in our lives, if we're open to receiving them."

"I'm not sure, Geula," I said, "but I think I did something sort of like that this morning. Before I came here I was dunking my feet in the brook, and doing a 'thought experiment' like you taught me. I imagined myself swimming in the water at the Douglaston beach, and then all of a sudden, you and Mariel were in my mind at the beach with me. Mariel and I were playing in the water and you were sitting on a navy blanket. And then I got here this morning and now everything is happening the way I saw it in my mind."

Geula nodded and grinned the whole time I was talking, then said, "Amazing! You got an answer about the beach even before I did. See? Didn't I tell you that mind of yours is capable of doing things that, even in your wildest dreams, you couldn't begin to imagine?"

"Is that all there is to getting information?" I asked, let down that there wasn't more mystery to it.

Geula glanced at me, then said, "You look disappointed, but you know there are all kinds of ways to get information that I haven't taught you about yet. Do you want to hear about them?"

"Like what kind?" I asked, interested again.

"Well . . . altogether there are four receivers inside of you that you can use to bring in information. The first one you already used today. That's the one where you get visual information, where you actually see images or mental pictures in your head with what is called your 'mind's eye.' That's the spot in the middle of your forehead between your two eyes," she said, touching the place with her finger. "Another name for it is your third eye."

I touched my third eye spot to make sure I understood. Geula watched, then said, "That's it. Good."

"Or," she continued, "you can listen to the words that you hear inside your head, like when I asked if the beach water was clean, and heard the word 'Yes.'

"Or you can tune into the feelings that talk to you in here." She tapped the place between her chest and stomach.

"Aren't those called your 'gut feelings'?" I asked, already knowing I was right.

"Yes they are," Geula answered, then said, "now there's one more. Can you think of another place on your body that might be a receiver for information?"

I thought hard for a moment, but nothing came to me.

"I can't think of any, Geula," I answered, quickly giving up so she would tell me.

"That's okay. It's a hard question. It's the top of your head," she said, pointing. "With this receiver you absolutely, definitely know something without knowing how you know it or why. The name for that receiver is called your 'inner knowing.' I use this one a lot, but all four of these receivers will bring information into you from everywhere."

Geula weighed her next words carefully. "Now, this is most important of all. When you get this information, trust it as the complete truth of what you need, and honor and follow the answers you get.

"Can you do that?" Geula looked at me intently.

I nodded, then said, "I think I can do what you say, Geula, but I have a question. How do I know when I listen to my receivers that I'm not making the information up myself? How do I know that it's really being given to me?"

Geula listened. "Don't worry about it or try to figure out where the information is coming from. It doesn't really matter. Just trust and keep those receivers open because whatever information is coming to you and in whatever form it comes, none of it is accidental. Everything you get is for a purpose.

"Remember that blind faith we talked about?"

I nodded.

"Good," Geula said, smiling. "Well, this is one of those times to use it. Now. How would you like to learn to use your mind and body to make the right decisions for you?"

"Yeah, I would. How?" I quickly answered.

"First, think about some situation in which you can't decide what to do." Geula waited until I motioned that I had the situation in mind.

"Okay. Now ask yourself, Should I do this or should I do that?, and wait for your answer by the feelings and physical reactions that come up inside of you. You can tell if something is good or bad for you by using your whole body as a barometer.

"If you question your decision and your body reacts with a signal that says, 'This doesn't feel right,' and you get nervous or have doubts or an uneasy feeling all over, trust it. Believe me, your body knows better than your logic does. That feeling is the signal for 'No, stop. Don't do it. You'll be sorry you didn't listen.'

"But, on the other hand, if your body feels relaxed or strong or sure inside, then that's the signal for 'Yes. Go for it. You're doing the right thing.'"

Geula looked directly at me. "Do you understand?"

"Yes," I answered. "I've already had those signals lots of times. Only I don't always listen to them. Especially when I really want to do something badly. Even though my insides say loud and clear, 'Don't!' I ignore them and do what I want anyway. Usually, it ends up causing me a big problem that I'm sorry for. And then afterwards I tell myself I should have listened to my feelings, but I never do.

"Stupid, huh?"

Geula smiled. "Not really. Just human. Most people do the same thing. That's how they get themselves into so many messes. It isn't always easy to give up doing what you want, especially if another choice isn't as immediately fulfilling, or there doesn't seem to be another good choice at the moment. If people would only listen to their inner signals and tune into information from their receivers, and not act, and wait it out, they would find that the right answer will absolutely come along when the time is right."

Geula's expression suddenly became serious. "The hardest thing for people is to wait until the time is right. That's why they push for solutions or make up their own answers.

"Timing is everything," Geula stressed. "If you were to get the information you wanted too early, you wouldn't know what it meant or how to use it. It is very important to wait until all the pieces come together for everything to make sense. Sometimes even months and years have to go by. But it's worth the wait because then everything will happen exactly the way it's supposed to."

Then Geula's tone softened and she smiled at me. "Just keep on trusting all your information receivers and your signals. Believe me, you'll know everything at the right time. I promise.

Okay?"

"Okay," I answered, smiling back.

Geula looked down at her watch.

"Oh my gosh, 11:30! My inner receivers are telling me we're going to miss the tide if we don't hurry. Go put on the bathing suit that Mariel has laid out on the bed for you."

I was about to ask Geula how she knew it was on the bed, since we had been talking the whole time Mariel was upstairs getting ready, but why bother asking? The answer was obvious.

Now it was my turn to use my receivers.

I walked from the kitchen to the bottom of the staircase, took a few deep breaths and closed my eyes.

In my mind I got the mental picture of Mariel's bed covered with the burgundy-red chenille spread. "Get closer and look at the bathing suit," I told myself. My mind zoomed in for a closer look. There it was, a tiger-printed one-piece bathing suit. I waited for more and a definite inner knowing came in and confirmed what I saw.

I opened my eyes. All right! I just got information on two of my receivers. Now all I have to do is check it out for accuracy.

"Mariel," I called out, "I'm coming up to get into my suit. The tiger one. Right?"

"How did you know?" she called back from her room.

"I just knew," I answered smugly.

Well, Geula, I thought, if I got this information so easily, maybe I won't have a hard time getting my answers about you.

The Right Decision

The hours went by far too quickly. I still couldn't believe that I actually swam at the Douglaston beach—and with the permission of a grown-up! If my parents ever found out that I went to the beach and that Geula used her receivers to ask God if the water was clean, they would be furious with me, probably think she was nuts, and not allow me to go to that incredible house ever again.

I left the Franklins' backyard by way of the path into the woods and headed for the brook, since my mind seemed to work best there. Maybe it was because the forest was so quiet, or maybe it was the sound of the rushing water. Either way, I needed the time to be alone, to think.

I pushed my way between the tangled honeysuckle vines that had wrapped themselves around the mountain laurels, stepping on the overgrown ferns, and made my way to my most favorite spot by the brook, the concrete culvert. The water was the loudest and most gurgling there, and the sound had a way of lulling me into a kind of hypnotic trance, helping me relax and focus my thoughts on Geula.

From the very first moment we met, I knew there was something very unusual about her. And after what Geula had taught me today, no doubt I picked up about her on my different information receivers. Not only did I know it in my mind, but in different parts of my body too. I felt it inside my chest and my gut, and sometimes when she spoke to me, I had goose bumps all over my arms and legs. Even the hair on the back of my neck stood on end. There was no doubt in my mind that she had to be someone special because no one else made me react this way. Ever.

To look at her no one could tell anything because she didn't look any different from the women in my life, except for two things: her incredible piercing eyes that seemed to look right into you, and her dresses. Geula always wore the same kind of dress, the same shirtwaist style and always in blue. Every day she put on a different shade of blue. And when I asked her why she did it, she just smiled her same familiar smile, stared up at the sky, and said, "Look up. See how pale the sky is today? Almost white. Yesterday, it was so bright blue, it almost looked like Florida water. And last night, it turned almost navy. Aren't all the blues of the sky wonderful?"

Then she went on. "Life can be so exciting when you learn to tune into every tiny change, and look at all of it as if you're seeing it for the first time.

"I never take any experience for granted. They are all gifts from the universe to us. That's why I wear a different blue dress every day. It's to remind me of the ever-changing sky and to always see the specialness of all things with fresh eyes."

I loved when Geula spoke that way to me. She took time, seemed to like to tell me reasons, and never dismissed my questions as if I were annoying her. I felt closer to Geula in only a few days than I had to my parents my whole life.

If only I could go home and tell them about her, our first meeting, and how amazing she was today. But how could I? I would be setting myself up for a problem I didn't need. Whenever I did talk to them, I had to think about everything I wanted to say before it came out of my mouth. And always leave out any topics they might react badly to.

And even though Geula had told me to trust, I couldn't quite bring myself to do so with them. Or with anyone for that matter. Even with her.

Yet what choice did I have?

I had to get an answer to my secret. I had carried it around too long. Not even my two best friends from the Bronx knew, and we shared just about everything. I was desperate to get it out once and for all and make some sense of what happened. If anyone could understand, it was Geula.

Besides, it probably was only a matter of time anyway. After all, she did have a way of knowing things even before she was told, not to mention she was also an expert on using her receivers to get information.

Maybe it would be better in the long run to tell her before she found out on her own.

Possibly tomorrow I would use my blind faith and take a chance on Geula. I wanted to so badly, but I still wasn't sure. Should I or shouldn't I?

I stood up still in a dilemma and walked toward the sunlight. The warmth of the day felt good on my body as I slowly made my way out of the cool, dark forest. Bright yellow goldenrod was growing everywhere in the meadow and I was surrounded by it as I stepped from the softness of the forest grasses onto the hot pavement.

The afternoon sun cast long shadows on the black-tarred road as I trudged toward home. This trip from the Franklins' had become so familiar to me that I didn't need to look ahead. Instead I kept my eyes on the pavement and thought more about Geula. Suddenly, as if from outer space, I heard Geula's voice inside me, no doubt coming from one of my information receivers.

"Use your mind and body to make the right decision for you," I heard her say in my mind.

"I forgot about that," I answered back out loud, suddenly feeling good that I was getting some direction.

Okay, remember what Geula told you to do. First ask the question.

"Should I or shouldn't I trust Geula and tell her about my secret?" I asked inside my mind.

I didn't have to wait more than a moment before I got the signal as clear as day. Actually it felt more like a surge of energy and a sure feeling of excitement.

"The answer is 'Yes'!" I yelled out. I looked around to see if anyone heard me. Luckily, nobody was in sight.

"Yes," I yelled again even louder. "I'll tell her tomorrow." I was so busy yelling and thinking, that without realizing it, I had passed Mrs. Johnson's house. Next was the Amideos. Then mine.

"Yes." I whispered . . . "Tomorrow."

YES TO THE UPS AND DOWNS

Somehow the next morning, the surge of energy and the confidence I felt only yesterday afternoon had disappeared, leaving me with the same mounting fear and self-doubt that I thought had gone away.

Even though I didn't want to go, I forced myself to walk the road to the Franklins', worrying with each step what would happen.

My secret was no little thing. What if, after I told Geula, she rejected me or worse yet, thought I was a liar? Could I take that chance?

Yet there seemed to be no other choice. I had to get my answers and Geula was the only one who might possibly understand what had happened to me. Besides, she was the one who stressed how important it is to trust. And I did what she said. I trusted someone to send me a signal and I got the one that said, "Go ahead." She couldn't get mad at me for following what she had told me to do in the first place.

Talking to myself calmed my nerves a bit as I walked to their house, chanting "trust and blind faith, trust and blind faith, trust and blind faith." Repeating the words over and over diverted my attention from the knot in my stomach and the pounding of my heart, and kept my mind occupied until I reached their front door.

I took a deep breath. It was now or never. I knocked loudly. No answer.

"Leave now and she'll never know you were here," a little voice inside me urged.

"No way. Forget it," I answered back.

I knocked again and turned the knob. Maybe they were upstairs or in the basement and couldn't hear me and wouldn't mind if I let myself in.

Geula was stretched out on the yellow-flowered couch on the sun porch, sound asleep. No wonder she hadn't answered my knock. As I tiptoed closer, trying to decide what to do, Geula spoke.

"Good morning, Ivy. Mariel's in her room. Go on up."

I was startled by her voice and, even more so, that she knew it was me standing there. Her eyes were still closed, so how did she know?

I moved closer to the couch.

"I'm sorry I woke you," I began to explain.

Geula opened her eyes and sat up.

"No need to apologize. I wasn't really sleeping, I was meditating. Although I do know everything going on around me, even with my eyes shut."

I was hardly listening. Getting my secret out was all that I could think about.

"Geula . . .," I stammered, "I came this morning because I have to talk to you. Something very weird happened to me when I was living in the Bronx. It happened a few months before we moved here, to Douglaston."

I paused, afraid to continue, but forced myself to go on. "I never told anybody about it because I was too ashamed. But since I met you, and you know so much about strange things, I figured maybe you could help me."

I took a deep breath. There it was, out in the open. No turning back now. I stood motionless and waited for Geula's response.

Geula didn't blink an eye, like it was going to be anything horrible. Instead she tapped the couch cushion, and gently said, "Sit down next to me and tell me all about it. Then I'll see what I can do."

I nodded and sat down.

I was still very nervous about telling her, but her encouragement and kind voice calmed me and made it a little easier to start. My face was red with embarrassment, so to hide my feelings, I looked down at my lap.

"Well, ever since I was four or five," I began hesitantly, "I felt like an outcast, different from the other kids my age. I looked normal like them on the outside, but my mind was always filled with different kinds of thoughts all the time, and my interests weren't like anyone else's I knew."

"In what way?" Geula questioned.

I looked up at Geula to check how she was reacting so far to the little I had told her already. Her expression showed no judgment, only genuine concern. So I took a deep breath and continued.

"When the other girls in the neighborhood were together playing house and dressing their dolls, the way you're supposed to do when you're that age, I liked being alone, sitting on the linoleum map of the United States on my bedroom floor learning the capitals of the states. And I loved spending hours memorizing poetry, especially Ogden Nash's poems. But my most different activity was this game I made up. I would kneel in front of my parents' bookcase and stare at their set of the 'Wonderland Books of Knowledge.' Then I'd wait until something inside me would say, 'Take that book.' I would grab the book I was supposed to, let's say the "A" book, and hold it until the same something inside would tell me, 'Open it to this page because there's something in it for you to learn today.' Then I'd open the book and read what was on that particular page. I really believed that whatever page came up was important information that I was supposed to know for some reason.

"This game was fun and seemed normal to me, but I didn't see anybody else do it or ever talk about reading books this way. Not my parents. Not any of my friends or the kids at school mentioned anything like it. Nobody! And that's just one of the things that proved that I was different from everyone else.

"That's not my secret though. I just wanted you to know all the ways that I feel like a misfit."

I glanced again at Geula for a reaction. She had the same calm, interested expression, so I went on. "First, before I tell you my secret, I have to tell you what my house in the Bronx looked like so you'll be able to picture what I'm talking about. Because that's where it happened."

Geula nodded for me to go on, so I began talking again.

"We lived in this three-story brownstone that my Grandpa Shea owned. He rented out the top floor to Mr. Reizel, the egg candler. Grandma, Grandpa, and Aunt Daisy lived together in the second-floor apartment, and my parents and I lived on the ground floor.

"Every morning, I would leave my apartment, walk down the hallway, and climb this huge, wide, rubber-treaded staircase going up from my floor to my grandparents' and have breakfast with my grandma in her kitchen."

Suddenly, I grew anxious, so I stopped talking and took a

breath. Telling secrets felt dangerous to me, even if it was to someone as safe and caring as Geula.

Geula must have sensed my difficulty because she leaned over and gently patted my hand.

"Don't worry about anything," she said. "I know this isn't easy for you, but keep going. It'll be okay. I promise."

Her reassuring words and easy manner helped take the edge off the fear growing in my stomach. And since I knew I had no choice but to go on, I took another breath and continued.

"Well, one night, I had this unbelievable dream. It took place in the same hallway and on the same staircase that I just told you about.

"It was nighttime in my dream, and I saw myself sleeping in my bed. Then all of a sudden, I watched me wake up, get out of bed, and walk out of my room. I opened my apartment door and walked down the hallway to the staircase. I held onto the big oak banister and climbed the stairs to the floor my grandparents lived on, but I didn't go into their apartment. Instead, when I reached the second-floor landing, I watched myself turn and look down the staircase toward the front door that led out to the street in front of my house.

"Then I saw myself do the most unbelievable thing. I gave a little push off the floor, and floated down the stairs. And landed lightly on my feet like a glider plane.

"This same dream kept coming back to me over and over, and each time I had this dream, the flying seemed more and more real. And it wasn't just there with me at night. Even while I was awake and playing during the day, the dream would still be there in my mind.

"And the more the dream was there, the more I became sure that it wasn't really a dream after all, but that somehow I had actually flown down that staircase at night. I convinced myself that since I had done it so easily at night so many times, and so successfully, that it was time to test it out in the daytime, to see if I could really fly like that when I was fully awake and could check it out for myself.

"The first thing I had to do was to make sure that my test flight would take place when everyone in the house was either busy doing something in their apartments or away at work. I didn't want to take the chance of getting caught in midflight or when I was landing at the bottom of the staircase. How could I explain to anyone that flying down the stairs was normal?

"So when I was sure the timing was right, I slowly climbed the stairs, absolutely believing I would fly. With each step I thought about all my successful nighttime flights. When I reached the second-floor landing, I stood at the exact spot and remembered all the details and feelings of my flying. Then, like I had seen myself do so many times in my dream, I pushed for a liftoff.

"It should have gone perfectly, but instead of gliding and gently landing on my feet, I was falling. Too fast to grab onto the banister. Out of control, I fell down each step, and didn't stop until I hit the floor below.

"I got up really fast and looked around. I felt so stupid and confused and angry with myself. Instead of flying, I had fallen down the whole flight of stairs and hurt myself. I was so ashamed that I didn't pay any attention to how scraped up I was.

"How could I fail? I had seen myself flying so easily over and over. And not once had I fallen. Just gliding and landing. So how was it possible to fly at night and not be able to do it in the daytime? Maybe it was only a dream, but it felt so real and so right to follow it.

"And that's why I was embarrassed to tell anyone about my

secret. I feel ashamed telling you about it even now."

"Did you ever have that dream again after the day you fell?" she questioned, looking directly into my eyes.

"No. Never again. Probably because I learned the difference between dreaming and reality. Even if I did dream it, I would know better than to ever try flying again."

"What do you think would have happened if you didn't fall and flew down the stairs as you believed you could?," she persisted, still watching me.

"I would do it again. But that didn't happen and I learned my lesson, once and for all," I admitted, looking down in shame.

I fully expected Geula to agree, but to my surprise she seemed upset with me. "Don't ever say those words again." Her voice was raised. "Don't let yourself even think that way. You're wiping out the terrific risk you took trying to make your dream a reality." Then noticing the scared and shocked look on my face, her voice suddenly softened and she smiled.

"Honey, I'm not angry at you. It's just that I don't want you to ever even think about giving up on any of your dreams.

"Without them, and belief and hope, life is worth nothing. You must have dreams . . . lots and lots of them. And keep trying them out, because some of your ideas, with time and hard work, you'll be able to make happen."

She hesitated for a moment, then went on. "But let me warn you. There will be other times, that no matter how much energy and thought you put into your dreams, it won't work out. Not because of lack of desire or effort on your part, but because not everything we dream always happens in our lifetime. Sometimes an important piece is missing. And we either have to discover it for ourselves with more experimentation or more knowledge if possible, or wait for someone else with other information or technology to discover it for us. Possibly not for years, or even centuries."

She looked at me intensely and said, "Maybe you weren't able to fly, but it could be you set the groundwork for someone else to do it. What if one day in the future someone has the same dream and based on your experimenting and because there is more advanced technology, is able to do it? How would you feel then? Stupid or embarrassed still?"

I shook my head vehemently. "No, of course not. I'd feel smart that I thought of something important."

"Good," she said, nodding, "and that's the way you should feel about yourself right now! Whether someone takes your experience to the next level or not doesn't mean it wasn't valuable or worth dreaming. By trying to live out your dream you already gave the world something beneficial. Who knows what the future will hold? Maybe you already did some necessary groundbreaking and just aren't aware of it.

"That's how all of our inventions and medical breakthroughs came about. Behind a lot of outstanding successes, there were many dreamers, who for whatever reason, couldn't take it to the final step, but who gave guidance and hope to others so that they could.

"Do you remember when we talked about your feather and I told you about Daedalus and the wings he created out of wax and feathers? And that centuries later Leonardo da Vinci's sketches showed a man with large wings attached to his shoulders flying?"

As I nodded, she continued. "Well, when da Vinci died, not only did he leave behind designs for a flying machine, but he also left behind sketches of propellers, helicopters, and parachutes. He even created a machine gun and an armored vehicle similar to the tanks our soldiers are using in the war now. He understood principles about machines that weren't put to use until hundreds of years after his death."

Geula leaned closer to me. "Remember, no dream is ever wasted," she stressed. "What we don't understand today will make perfect sense tomorrow. Da Vinci designed the dream and the Wright brothers went even further, 300 years later, and created a power-driven flying machine. Which, by the way, Orville flew just 120 feet for only 12 seconds. Each person's dream led us up to the airplane we know today.

"So because da Vinci didn't see any of his designs in action would you call his work a failure? Would you call him a foolish dreamer?"

I was shocked by Geula's questions. "Are you kidding? Of course not! Everyone knows he was a genius."

Geula smiled at me and said, "And so are you and all those people who dare to dream and then attempt to bring those dreams into reality.

"Our world has always depended on dreams and dreamers for just about everything. After all, where would we be today without some caveman who got tired of walking and looked at a rock and dreamed of a wheel?" Then, with an amused look on her face, she added, "I'll bet he cracked a lot of rocks and made many odd-shaped wheels that didn't work.

"When it comes to dreaming and taking chances on those dreams, there are no failures, only steps and outcomes, even if things don't work out the way you wanted. And I don't mean just taking chances on only what you're doing; I mean taking chances on yourself."

I frowned, not quite sure what she was getting at.

Geula picked up on my confusion immediately, then said, "Let's see if I can explain it more clearly. Remember how discouraged you were when your flying experiment didn't work out?"

I nodded, listening.

"Well, most people react the same as you. Some even blame other people and circumstances for their frustration and pain, and complain endlessly, but do very little to change anything. They usually end up believing they have a right to be disappointed and sorry for themselves."

Geula's voice had a tone of annoyance. "What a waste of time, energy, and talent that could be put to better use! I mean, look at all the famous people that overcame problems. The very reason we know about them and their fame is because they didn't give up."

Suddenly her eyes brightened. "I mean, look at Walt Disney."

My interest immediately piqued at the mention of his name.

"Everyone takes his wonderful animated movies and Mickey Mouse for granted. That he's talented and that everything is easy for him." Geula snickered. "Let me tell you, that's not true. He had plenty of setbacks in his life."

"Like what, Geula?" I couldn't believe that someone as famous as Walt Disney could possibly have any problems.

"Well," Geula answered, "to begin with, as a young man he had his heart set on becoming a political cartoonist. He tried to get a job everywhere, and couldn't get one. He was very unhappy, but accepted his disappointment and went to work drawing at an advertising company.

"And guess what? This job didn't last very long either. Already in his young life, two jobs he wanted didn't pan out.

"Walt didn't become a political cartoonist, and he lost the second job, but what he did gain is what happens when you trust the experience even though you don't understand the reasons why, and say 'Yes' to those ups and downs of life."

"What good is that?" I interrupted. "It looks to me like he lost two good jobs. I don't see that he gained anything."

"I beg to differ with you," she quickly snapped back. "What he gained is a belief in himself, no matter what the outcome. Let's face it, it's easy to say 'yes' when things work out exactly the way you want them to. But it's a whole lot harder to have belief and say 'yes' when things don't work out the way you expect."

"Personally," I interjected, "I'd rather say 'no.'"

Geula responded quickly. "Unfortunately, that's why most people give up so easily and never achieve their dreams.

"The most important thing in life is to say 'yes' especially to the downs and disappointments. You have to trust and accept the experience for whatever lessons or gains that will come out of it, and not curse it or stop yourself."

Geula touched my arm to emphasize her point. "Everything in life happens for a reason. That's why I'm telling you that you must trust and accept whatever happens unconditionally and wait with an open mind.

"Because you know what? That's what Walt did, and let me tell you, it paid off. His next job was for a film ad company that made one-minute animated commercials that were shown in local movie houses. And that changed his life forever.

"In fact, he like animation so much that he talked his friend, Ubbe, into moving to Hollywood to open up a movie studio."

"And then he was successful," I added.

"Not exactly," Geula corrected. "Everything seemed to be going well for the new Disney Studio, when one day, his film distributor suggested that Walt create a new animated film with a rabbit as its main character. So Walt designed Oswald the Rabbit, but what Walt didn't know was that he didn't own the rights to Oswald. The distributor did. And when the Oswald movies became very successful, the distributor did something sneaky. He hired away the artists who drew Oswald, and there was Walt, stuck with no artists and no Oswald!"

"That's not fair," I protested. "No way could he say 'yes' to this down. This is the worst."

Geula nodded, then said empathetically, "You're right. Sometimes life is very unfair. Difficult things happen to us that we can't change. And no amount of wishing will make them go away. But what does help is hope and believing in yourself, even when the situation is the worst. Saying 'yes' to those down times is the only thing that helps because it gives you some kind of control over the situation.

"It also helps if you ask yourself, What can I learn from what just happened to me? Or, what can I do with this experience to help myself? Or, what can I do to at least make myself feel better inside even if I can't change anything on the outside?"

"Okay, Geula," I questioned. "But even if Walt understood, wasn't he still frustrated and angry at what happened?"

"Of course, he was," Geula replied. "How could he not be? After all, he had normal feelings like everyone else. And if he chose to, he could have easily used his loss as an excuse to give up, but he still believed in himself. He thought, 'They took Oswald from me, but no one can take away my creative abilities. And if I made a successful character once, nothing can stop me from doing it again.'"

Geula continued. "As Walt sat thinking about how he would create a new character, a picture popped into his mind. He remembered from one of his jobs a pet mouse that he fed crumbs and had trained to do tricks. Then, out of nowhere, like a flash it hit him. 'I'll bet the public would love a cartoon about a mouse.' And you know who that turned out to be, don't you?"

"Mickey!" I shouted, excitedly.

"Right!" Geula smiled back at me. "And that was to reward Walt for say 'yes' and trusting the experience, and for believing in himself and never giving up."

Suddenly her face turned serious. "Isn't it strange that so many people look up to Walt Disney and all the other famous people, yet don't take chances on their own abilities?"

I nodded. "That's a good question, Geula. Why don't they?"

"Because they don't think they're good enough and because they're afraid."

"That doesn't make any sense at all," I argued. "They're grown-ups. They can do anything they want. Nobody's stopping them. So what could they be scared of?"

Geula took a breath. "Sadly, they're afraid to take risks because maybe they could fail. So out of their fear, they settle for a life of security. They hang on for safety instead of letting go and reaching for what they want."

She paused, then added, "I think what the real problem is, they don't have enough belief in themselves and their abilities to take chances. That's too bad, because if they did take the chance and really wanted it to work out, there would be all kinds of answers and possibilities everywhere."

I was silent for a moment as I thought about my father, feeling sorry for him, then said, "My father wanted to be an architect, but instead he works in the garment center."

Geula shook her head sadly. "It's too bad he didn't do what he wanted. So many people like him hold themselves back, sacrifice their dreams, and never try to find their purpose—the real reason why they're here on this earth."

Her words intrigued me, so I asked, "What am I here for, Geula? I don't know yet."

Geula looked at me thoughtfully, and paused for what seemed a very long time as if she were trying to get information from her receivers.

"I don't know yet, either," she said at last, "but one think I do know for sure. You already have begun preparation for your purpose, just by the things you've told me up to now."

"Like what?" I persisted.

"Like the way you read those 'Wonderland Books of Knowledge,' seeking out information, or the way you tested your flying dream. It looks to me like you're curious and will go anywhere and do anything to investigate for more information."

Geula paused, looking somehow worried. "But be aware," she went on, "that because of the fears that most grown-ups have, they will spend a lot of time and effort convincing you of what you can't and shouldn't do. How you should think the way everyone else does, and behave yourself and live the 'right way.' They will use whatever they can to stop you with the same reasoning they use to stop themselves."

I nodded as she spoke, then said reassuringly, "That's okay, Geula, I make up my own mind now, only I don't let my parents know about it."

"That's too bad that you can't be honest with them, but I'm glad that you're learning to think for yourself. Still, be careful not to fall into all the fears and restrictions of those around you. Fear can be contagious if you don't protect yourself against it."

"I will," I said, understanding and agreeing completely.

All the while Geula was talking I was wondering whether to ask her something personal about her behavior, then decided it would probably be okay. I hesitated for a moment, trying to figure out how to begin, then said, "Geula, aren't you afraid that people will think you're weird because you do 'God bless' exercises and get information from your receivers? I don't know anybody that's like you or does what you do."

Geula reached over and patted my hand. "Sometimes I'm concerned. But I don't have any other choice. I live by my beliefs. They're my whole life and teaching them to you and Mariel or any-body else who wants to learn feels like my special purpose for being here."

"But no one would hurt you, would they, Geula?" I pressed, suddenly distressed.

Geula patted my hand again, trying to put my mind at ease, "Don't worry. The worst that would happen is that I'll be laughed at, but I'll still keep on with my work, no matter what.

"After all, aren't we all here to leave this world a better place than we found it?"

"I hope so. But how can I do it?" I asked.

"It's really easy," Geula said, smiling.

"Just learn as much as you can. Use that wonderful mind of yours and search out whatever grabs your interest, examine and question everything, and if you're not satisfied with the answers, look for new ones. Keep going. Use your energy to create and to push you to make things work. And always remember to say 'Yes' to everything, especially the downs.

"But most of all, have faith in your dreams and abilities. Never, never give up on yourself, no matter what."

Geula paused a moment, then added, "I like to think that life is an adventure, and sometimes the adventure gives you some sur-prising outcomes that are better than what you could have ever imagined or planned for yourself.

"And if you live every day that way, eventually you'll find your special purpose.

"So," Geula said, smiling, "do you think you can follow what I just said?"

"Absolutely," I said, feeling full of energy.

Geula stood up. "Good! Oh, and by the way, how do you feel

now about your flying secret?"

I grinned broadly. "Are you kidding? Proud of myself. Thank you, Geula."

"You're welcome," she said warmly, walking toward the kitchen, "and I hope you have a good appetite this morning because it's time to fix you and Mariel some breakfast. How does Corn Flakes with bananas sound to you?"

My mouth watered. "Delicious!"

"Good," she said over her shoulder. "Go call Mariel."

I walked to the foot of the staircase, and inside thought, "I promise, I'll follow it for the rest of my life," then yelled out loud, "Hey, Mariel, your mother's making breakfast. Come on down."

HEALING AND THE MIND

The day flew by. I walked home from the Franklin house, lost in my thoughts. I loved the freedom I had with Mariel and Geula and hated going home. At their house I was allowed to be myself, completely, as is. With them I felt like I was really free to fly, just like the beautiful butterflies I saw in their yard. But when I went home I had to change back and crawl like the ordinary caterpillar my parents expected me to be.

After Geula's talk about my special purpose, it wasn't going to be so easy to be the passive, good girl I was trained to be. And if I was going to find out what my purpose was, now was as good a time as any to begin challenging everything I didn't like or agree with. Not to make a big deal out of it or rebel in some major way, just to do what I believed in my heart was right. And what felt right for me now was to introduce my sister, Carly, to Geula. Besides, I had to get her away from home and out of the trouble she inevitably seemed to get herself into.

By the time I was two and a half, I somehow understood what my mother and father required of me, and I learned pretty quickly to do whatever was needed to make it through each day without problems or punishment.

My three-year-old sister, Carly, was not as devious or self-protective as I was. She was naive and honest—usually two good traits in a person, but unfortunately, Carly was too naive to know when to stop being honest, and in our family that kind of openness was very dangerous. Somehow she always seemed to be at fault for some kind of problem, especially with our mother.

Even before Carly was born, I overheard my mother complaining about her. First she griped that her whole pregnancy was terrible. Then I heard how awful giving birth to Carly was.

From the day Carly was brought home, my mother labeled her a born troublemaker. When Carly nursed, she couldn't hold down her formula and was either throwing up or cheesing, making a smelly cottage-cheese-like spit-up. My mother blamed her for having an undeveloped stomach, whatever that was. So poor Carly cried a lot and had to be fed often.

Then, when Carly was six months old, she got scarlet fever. And when her baby teeth came in, most of them were soft and rotten. Another irritation for my mother. She had to take Carly to Dr. Paul, the dentist, so he could paint fluoride on her teeth, hopefully to harden them.

Whenever my mother grumbled about what a problem child Carly was, I was glad. "Good," I thought, "she doesn't like her because she's a nuisance, but she loves me because I'm no trouble at all." My thoughts made me feel guilty, however, and responsible for Carly's unhappiness. I wanted to be an only child and hated sharing my family with my sister. How could there be enough love or attention for both of us? It already felt like love was in short supply.

I hated it when my parents said anything good about Carly, and felt worse when they were mean or hit her. What a rotten spot for me, caught between my jealousy and my guilt. And my parents were no help with my problem either. Not that they ever recognized that I had one. After all, I was just a kid, and only adults had feelings and difficulties worthy of consideration.

But that wasn't true. Like them, I needed to talk, and have someone understand and love me, and so did Carly. It was sad to think that I got more from Geula in a few short days than I had gotten from my parents my whole life. And if I brought Carly with me, maybe Geula would show her the love and attention she so desperately needed from a mother, which I couldn't give and really didn't want to.

In the pit of my stomach, I had grave doubts. It would be great for Carly to meet Geula and finally be happy. But what if when my parents asked her about her day, she told them all about Geula's strange ideas and the "God bless" exercises we did? After all, she was only three years old and way too honest for our good. Would it be smart to take such a risk?

As I approached my house I could hear Carly crying. Knowing her, odds were she had either gotten into trouble aggravating my mother, or had been whacked by Timmy Reilly's sister, Patsy. Being teased or hit by the Reillys happened on a daily basis. And I was getting tired of defending Carly against them or keeping her out of our mother's way. No doubt it would be easier for both of us if I took her with me to Geula's, but what about that gnawing feeling in my stomach? Maybe that was the answer signal Geula told me to pay attention to. After a few seconds, my mind quickly dismissed the feeling and I decided that if I talked to Carly and explained the rules she had to obey at the Franklins', everything would be okay.

I followed her cries to the bedroom we shared and found Carly sitting on her bed.

"Patsy told me I was a baby and couldn't play with her, then she hit me and ran inside her house," Carly whimpered. "Look at it." She held out her arm for me to see the red mark where Patsy had gotten her.

"Patsy's a brat. She only starts up with you when I'm not around. She's such a sneaky coward."

A smile quickly replaced Carly's tears. "Yeah, she's a sneaky coward. Are you going to get her back for me?"

"I have a better idea than to waste my time fighting with Patsy," I answered. "How would you like to come with me to play someplace tomorrow? This is a place I discovered and go to every day." I hesitated, then before what I really felt could get the better of me and talk me out of it, I blurted out, "It's a nice family that I found, and I go to their house to play. A girl named Mariel lives there and she has all kinds of comics, Looney Tunes and Woody Woodpecker. She has everything."

Carly's smile turned into a huge grin. "Really? And you're going to take me?"

I didn't return her smile. Instead I put a very serious expression on my face. "On one condition: if you don't tell Mommy or Daddy anything that goes on there. You can say that we played games and had fun. But that's all. Do you understand what I'm saying? If you can do that, I'll take you. Otherwise, you'll have to stay home."

Carly nodded her head. "I'll only say we played games and had fun. That's all. Is that right, Ivy?"

"Yes," I was still worried. "Are you sure you can do it?"

Carly nodded again. "I promise. Cross my heart and hope to die. Stick a finger in my eye." She crossed her heart with her forefinger, and looked up at me, waiting for my answer.

I knew she didn't understand what any of that meant, but she knew that when you made a promise you weren't supposed to

Mommy later tonight that you're
doing her a favor by keeping you

>oth my hands on Carly's shoul-

taring into her eyes. "Remember,
the talking. Do you understand?"
ny grasp. "Yes," she whined, still

erstand?"
:ed up at me. "Yes!" she yelled.
left the room. I still wasn't sure
shut, even though she said yes.
nber something one minute and
would be okay. But would it?

All that night as I laid in bed, my mind wouldn't let me rest. That anxious, gnawing feeling refused to leave my stomach. And after too many hours lying there staring at the ceiling, I thought myself to sleep with the plan that if I kept Carly quiet and happy and stayed on top of her, everything would probably be fine.

I awakened to a mosquito buzzing in my ear and Carly kneeling by my bed, with her nose an inch away from my face.

"Did she say 'yes'? Can I go?"

I nodded, annoyed at her early intrusion and turned toward the wall, hoping Carly would get the idea that it wasn't time to get up yet. No such luck.

She crawled up the side of the bed near the wall and whispered loudly. "Can we go now?"

I reached down quickly and put my hand over her mouth.

"Shhh. You're talking too loudly. You'll wake up Mommy. Go

read a book. We'll go in a little while."

Carly got off the bed and took her Golden Encyclopedia from the bookcase. She sat down on the carpet next to my bed, and turned the pages quickly, hardly looking at them, and finished the book in less than five minutes.

"I'm done reading," she said. "Now can we go?"

She was hopeless and there was no point trying to reason with her. "Go pick out which shorts and T-shirt you want to wear today. And don't forget underpants and socks."

Stalling Carly was no easy job, but I didn't want to show up at the Franklins' too early. Especially with an unexpected visitor. I hadn't mentioned to either Mariel or Geula that I was thinking about bringing my sister, and hoped her tagging along wouldn't be a problem. After all, when they first met me they already knew I was coming, so maybe today they also knew about my bringing Carly and were waiting for us, I rationalized. The thought pushed me to get ready. Besides, it was useless trying to waste time by staying in bed any longer.

Carly was struggling to dress herself and from the looks of her battle with the pink-flowered shirt she picked out, she needed my help. I grabbed my dungaree shorts off the chair and took a clean white T-shirt out of my dresser. I slipped my bare feet into my white moccasins and went over to help Carly, who had gotten stuck attempting to get her arm into the sleeve.

Carly stood at attention while I straightened out her tangled shirt and pulled up her navy-blue boxer shorts. She handed me a pair of yellow socks and stuck her foot right in my face. "Here, put these on."

"Take another pair," I ordered. "They don't match your shirt and shorts."

"No. I like yellow. I want to wear these." Carly's voice was break it.

"Okay then," I said. "I'll tell Mommy later tonight that you're coming with me. It'll be like I'm doing her a favor by keeping you busy. She'll like that and agree."

I sat down on the bed, put both my hands on Carly's shoulders, and turned her toward me.

"Look at me," I said sternly, staring into her eyes. "Remember, not one word about going. I'll do the talking. Do you understand?"

Carly tried to squirm out of my grasp. "Yes," she whined, still struggling to get free.

I held on. "Do you really understand?"

She stopped moving and looked up at me. "Yes!" she yelled.

"All right." I let go of her and left the room. I still wasn't sure that Carly would keep her mouth shut, even though she said yes. It wasn't unusual for her to remember something one minute and forget it the next. I had to trust it would be okay. But would it?

All that night as I laid in bed, my mind wouldn't let me rest. That anxious, gnawing feeling refused to leave my stomach. And after too many hours lying there staring at the ceiling, I thought myself to sleep with the plan that if I kept Carly quiet and happy and stayed on top of her, everything would probably be fine.

I awakened to a mosquito buzzing in my ear and Carly kneeling by my bed, with her nose an inch away from my face.

"Did she say 'yes'? Can I go?"

I nodded, annoyed at her early intrusion and turned toward the wall, hoping Carly would get the idea that it wasn't time to get up yet. No such luck.

She crawled up the side of the bed near the wall and whispered loudly. "Can we go now?"

I reached down quickly and put my hand over her mouth.

"Shhh. You're talking too loudly. You'll wake up Mommy. Go

read a book. We'll go in a little while."

Carly got off the bed and took her Golden Encyclopedia from the bookcase. She sat down on the carpet next to my bed, and turned the pages quickly, hardly looking at them, and finished the book in less than five minutes.

"I'm done reading," she said. "Now can we go?"

She was hopeless and there was no point trying to reason with her. "Go pick out which shorts and T-shirt you want to wear today. And don't forget underpants and socks."

Stalling Carly was no easy job, but I didn't want to show up at the Franklins' too early. Especially with an unexpected visitor. I hadn't mentioned to either Mariel or Geula that I was thinking about bringing my sister, and hoped her tagging along wouldn't be a problem. After all, when they first met me they already knew I was coming, so maybe today they also knew about my bringing Carly and were waiting for us, I rationalized. The thought pushed me to get ready. Besides, it was useless trying to waste time by staying in bed any longer.

Carly was struggling to dress herself and from the looks of her battle with the pink-flowered shirt she picked out, she needed my help. I grabbed my dungaree shorts off the chair and took a clean white T-shirt out of my dresser. I slipped my bare feet into my white moccasins and went over to help Carly, who had gotten stuck attempting to get her arm into the sleeve.

Carly stood at attention while I straightened out her tangled shirt and pulled up her navy-blue boxer shorts. She handed me a pair of yellow socks and stuck her foot right in my face. "Here, put these on."

"Take another pair," I ordered. "They don't match your shirt and shorts."

"No. I like yellow. I want to wear these." Carly's voice was beginning to get loud again.

"Shhh. Go ahead, look like a jerk, it doesn't bother me." I grabbed her foot and pulled on her socks. Then I bent down, picked up her white sandal shoes that were by the side of the bed, and buckled them on.

"We're done. Let's go downstairs and I'll make a bowl of cereal for you. Remember: tiptoe so you don't wake up Mommy." I held Carly's hand until we reached the kitchen. She scrambled onto the bench of the breakfast nook and waited while I poured milk over her corn flakes.

"We'll go after I finish eating, right?" Carly mumbled, spooning another mouthful in.

I nodded and took a swallow of milk. I purposely didn't make any breakfast for myself. The runny, soft-boiled eggs that my mother forced me to eat cured me of ever eating breakfast at home again. Even if I made it myself.

When Carly finished, I quietly washed and dried Carly's bowl and spoon and my glass and put them away, leaving no sign of our being in the kitchen. That's the way my mother expected it. Perfect. No trace of humans.

"Carly, go wait outside on the front walk for me," I whispered.

She quickly obeyed, while I closed and locked the front door, and then double-checked it to make sure.

I took a deep breath. So far, so good.

"We're ready to go," I said. Carly looked up at me with a grin from ear to ear and slid her hand into mine.

"Remember you told me that Mariel had a bunch of Looney Tunes and Woody Woodpecker comics, so I'm going to read them all," she chattered excitedly. "Okay?"

I was concentrating on Geula's and Mariel's reaction to my showing up with Carly and didn't answer.

"Okay, Ivy?" she repeated. "You're not answering me. Answer me!" she said, raising her voice.

"Okay! Carly." I really wanted to tell her to shut up, but she was only a happy little kid and didn't know when to keep quiet.

I did my best to tune Carly out while we walked and buried myself in my thoughts of Geula. I was pretty good at tuning people out when they were boring or I didn't like what they had to say. My mother and father fit both categories. At home, I acted like I was there and listening when I really wasn't.

When we neared the Franklin house and turned up the driveway, Carly's hand tightened on mine and she became silent.

"We're here," she whispered.

I pulled open the screen door to the porch and motioned for Carly to follow me in. Because she was with me I didn't feel free to just walk in unannounced. I knocked extra loudly on the wood and glass French doors that separated the porch from the house, hoping that either Mariel or Geula would be able to hear me from wherever they were inside.

Carly could care less what I was doing. She already had her eyes on the comics and toys that were scattered all over the porch floor.

"Don't touch," I scolded as she was about to grab a comic off the top of a pile. "You'll get to read them soon. Just wait."

Carly looked up at me with her usual hurt, not understanding expression. "But why can't I read it now?"

"Because it's not polite until you meet Geula and Mariel, so wait and do what I tell you to do." I gave her my big sister condescending stare and she returned it with her usual victim look, which I purposely ignored. I knocked again, even harder this time. It felt like we were waiting forever, so I peeked through the lace curtains on the inside of the door to see if anyone had heard me. I could see the outline of Geula's body as she made her way toward the door and opened it.

"I'm so please you're here and so early too," she smiled broadly. But as quickly as her smile came, it vanished, and she abruptly stopped talking. Geula seemed frozen to the spot as she stood staring down at Carly.

My heart sank. I knew it. I shouldn't have brought Carly without getting permission, but how could I leave her home to get into trouble. I so wanted Geula's help.

Maybe if I apologized or explained about Carly. But looking at the expression on Geula's face, something inside told me to just stand there and be quiet. My stomach kept doing flip-flops waiting for Geula to talk. But she said nothing. Just silence.

Carly stood half-hidden behind me.

Geula continued to stare at Carly. Finally instead of talking, she looked up toward the ceiling the same way she did when she conducted the "God bless" exercises. After about a minute, Geula relaxed, appearing satisfied with whatever answer she got, and motioned us into the house. "Come in. Come in," she said. Her manner was warm and friendly again as if nothing unusual had just taken place.

I took a deep breath and let it out audibly as the knot in my stomach loosened up a little.

"This is my sister, Carly," I stammered, still somewhat nervous. "Is it okay that I brought her?

"I know who she is, and I'm so delighted she's here." Geula smiled at me as though pleased for some unknown reason.

It felt good to know that she wasn't angry with me for bringing Carly, but there was certainly something weird in the way Geula was acting. How come at first she was shocked and then unusually happy at Carly's being here? I was dying to know, but my insides told me to leave well enough alone.

Mariel must have heard our voices and came bounding down the stairs.

Geula excitedly turned toward her daughter as she came into the room.

"Mariel, today is so special. Look who's here . . . Carly."

Mariel didn't appear as thrilled as her mother and from the blank expression on her face it looked like she didn't know any more than I did about what Geula was saying. She just looked like she was happy that there were two friends to play with instead of one.

Carly grinned back at Geula, showing her little decayed teeth. And as I predicted, she was already loving all the attention Geula was showing her.

Mariel, eager to have a new friend to show her treasures to, immediately headed out to the porch. "Come on, Carly. Do you want to see my baby doll? She pees if you feed her a bottle of water. You want to see her do it?"

Carly put both her hands over her mouth and giggled as she followed Mariel. Geula just stood there, still smiling, watching both girls walk out the door. And me . . . all I wanted was some answers as to what was making Geula so charged up by Carly's visit.

"Bye, see you later, Geula," I said, smiling extra-sweetly, before leaving for the porch. I had to make sure that I was still important to Geula and that she wouldn't lose interest in me and drop me like a hot potato now that Carly was here and seemed so special.

Out on the porch Carly was running from the pile of comics, to the dolls, to the blocks, to the assorted toys, and back again to the comics. She was trying to play with everything at once. And who could blame her? We had nothing like this at home. It was kind of nice seeing her so happy and busy, providing of course, she didn't cause any trouble for me or get in my way.

After watching them a while, and satisfied that Carly and Mariel were engrossed in playing, I started painting a beautiful still life of a vase of daisies sitting on a blue tablecloth. Halfway through creating my masterpiece, Geula called us in to lunch.

What a time to interrupt, right in the middle of the flowers. Reluctantly, I put my paintbrush down, but only after a last dab on one of the daisy petals. I looked up at the clock over the sofa and couldn't believe it was noon already. Where did the time go? Only the grumbling in my stomach made me realize for the first time since I began painting just how hungry I really was.

Geula came through the door with a platter of egg salad sandwiches on white bread cut in her usual hors d'oeurve quarters and placed it on the glass-topped black wrought iron coffee table.

"My favorite!" Carly squealed with delight as she lunged for the plate. I caught her hand in midair before she could take one.

"Don't be a pig. Wait, until we sit down and the drinks come," I scolded. Carly gave me one of her victim looks, but behaved.

I pushed the comics off the glider so that we could all comfortably fit and waited for Geula to come back. About a minute later, she arrived carrying three little juice glasses in one hand and a bottle of milk in the other. She poured the milk and placed a full glass in front of each one of us.

"Dig in, girls."

Needless to say, Carly was the first one to have her hand on the sandwiches. Mariel and I weren't far behind her. We grabbed for them like we hadn't eaten in days and finished eating everything on the plate in less than ten minutes.

"Done!" Carly exclaimed, as she banged down her empty glass on the tabletop, and reached for a comic that was resting near her foot.

I shot her a look. "Not now. After eating we have to do our exercises, then you can play."

"But I don't want to do exercises," Carly whined in her usual cry-baby manner.

"It'll be over before you know it, and then you can play to your heart's content. Besides, you're going to like these exercises, they're fun," I lied, to quiet her.

Carly quickly gave in.

I took her hand as the three of us got up off the glider and walked into the living room. Mariel and I knelt down on the rug in our usual places, and I positioned Carly on her knees close to me.

"Keep very quiet and do exactly what I do," I leaned over and whispered, then added, "and don't ask any questions."

Geula came into the room and knelt down in our circle next to Mariel. "I see you're ready. Thank you," she said warmly. "Now let's all begin our exercises by breathing deeply." We took deep breaths to relax our bodies and began the regular "God bless" routine. First we closed our left eyes, squeezed, then opened them, for six times, then our right eyes, then both eyes. And each time we chanted "God bless my eye."

Carly silently watched and attempted to imitate everything we did as well as a three-year-old could. But when Geula added "God bless my teeth" to our exercises, in honor of Carly's decayed teeth, Carly grinned excitedly, showing her rotten teeth, and really got into it with even more effort.

And as annoyed as I was with all the special attention Carly was getting, I really couldn't blame her for wanting nice teeth. It had to be embarrassing for her to walk around with ugly teeth that everybody asked about or made fun of.

"If we talk to God, will my teeth turn white and not be broken anymore?" Carly cut in, no doubt wanting any help she could get.

I smirked, knowing Carly couldn't go for long without interrupting, no matter what the subject. However, the question she asked was a really good one, and personally, I was dying to know the answer to it myself, but didn't have the nerve to ask.

Geula sat silently for a few moments, staring at Carly.

"That's a very good question," she said finally, her expression changing as if she were pleased for some reason. Then she turned to me. "You wanted to know about the 'God bless' exercises when you first joined us and I remember saying 'one day you'll know.' Well, I can't think of a better day than today to talk about why we're doing them and how they actually work."

Geula leaned forward, smiling. "But before I tell you, let's begin by learning a trick."

"What kind of trick?" Carly piped up.

Geula smiled over at her, then got up from her place on the rug and stood in front of us. She beckoned with her hands.

"Come on. Stand up and I'll show you."

We scrambled to our feet and stood in a line in front of Geula.

"Are we going to do the trick now?" Carly asked insistently.

Geula looked down at her. "We sure are. Okay, girls, what I want you to do is put your right arm out straight to the side, like this, level with your shoulder." Geula put her arm out to demonstrate. All three of us, wanting to be able to do the trick properly, followed her directions precisely.

Geula checked us out. "Good. Now I want you to think of something that's exciting and fun, or something that happened that you have happy feelings and memories about."

"Like the Coney Island Amusement Park?" I interrupted. "There's a special merry-go-round that I love going on with my father. It's called the Derby Racer."

"How about my birthday party?" Mariel added.

"Yeah, a birthday party." Carly said happily, her big eyes lighting up at Mariel's words. It was obvious she didn't have a clue as to what was really going on, but the phrase "birthday party" struck a chord with her. And for sure that made her happy.

Geula laughed approvingly. "Perfect! That's it."

"That's it? That's the whole trick?" Mariel sounded annoyed, like she had been had by her mother and there wasn't some amazing finish to the trick.

"No," Geula quickly answered. "This is only a trial run before we do the real trick. You'll like it, I promise.

"Let's go on," Geula continued. "Keep your arm up and think the same happy things from before, only this time, close your eyes. And while you're thinking about Coney Island, or that birthday party, or whatever makes you happy, I will try to push your arm down. Remember, all you have to do is concentrate on feeling good, and not think about what your arm's doing." Then Geula looked at each one of us in turn. "Everybody understand?"

Mariel and I nodded. Carly, not to be left out, imitated by shaking her head too.

Geula turned to face me. "You and I will do it together first. Stand in front of me." I quickly did as Geula instructed.

"Good," she said. "Now, put your arm out, the same way you just practiced, and close your eyes. Take a deep breath, like when you do the 'God bless' exercises, and just relax."

I took an extra deep breath and stood there with my eyes closed and my right arm straight out to the side, waiting for Geula's next direction.

"Now," she directed softly, "think of that scene at Coney Island that you just mentioned, and I want you to let yourself feel as happy as you did when it happened in real life. See a picture of it in your mind. Imagine it as real as you can and that you're reliving it again, having lots and lots of fun."

I saw my father and me on the merry-go-round in Coney Island making believe we were racing our horses. He was trying to get ahead with his horse and I was laughing as mine came up and passed his. We were having the best time together. I could hear Geula's voice. "Keep your eyes closed and continue concentrating on the picture in your mind and how happy and good you feel while I try to push your arm down."

I felt her pushing, but for some reason my arm felt powerful and hardly moved under her pressure. In fact, when I was thinking about Coney Island and the fun my father and I were having, my whole body felt strong.

Geula's voice interrupted my thoughts. "Okay, now, open your eyes and put your arm down."

I did as she instructed while she turned her attention to Mariel.

"Now it's your turn, and after you, Carly."

I sat down on the rug and waited for her to do the same thing with Mariel and then Carly. She was doing it with Carly more not to leave her out.

"Is this the trick, Geula?" I asked. It was fun to do, but I agreed with Mariel, it didn't seem like much of a trick to me either.

"Only half of it," Geula said, motioning for me to stand in front of her again. "Now we'll do the rest of it.

"Put your arm out like you did before but this time, I want you to think of something that makes you miserable, something that upsets you or makes you feel helpless. Remember to get a picture of the scene clearly in your mind and when you're ready close your eyes."

I stood in front of Geula, put my arm out to the side, and closed my eyes. This time I saw myself back in the Bronx playing chase with my grandfather. I was kidding around and slammed the door in his face. For some dumb reason it turned from a game to him getting insulted. He lay down on his bed and wouldn't talk to me. My mother got mad and punished me, and said I was mean for hurting his feelings.

In my mind, I saw myself standing in front of my grandfather apologizing, and him still looking hurt. The guilty feeling that I had when it happened for real was as strong now as it was back then. Still deep in thought, I could hear Geula saying, "I'm going to push down on your arm, don't let me." The image of my grandfather's face and the feeling of total shame wouldn't leave my mind.

Through my daze I felt Geula pushing down on my arm, but strangely, this time instead of being strong like before, it was as limp as a rag doll's. My body had absolutely no energy.

"Now, open your eyes," Geula said, "and don't forget what just happened. After I do the trick with Mariel and Carly, we'll talk."

I sat back down on the rug and said nothing.

When Geula finished giving them each a turn, she also sat back down in her usual place on the rug. Mariel and Carly followed.

"So, girls, what do you think of that trick?" she asked.

I couldn't wait to talk. "That was pretty amazing, Geula, but I don't understand how it happened. How did my arm go from being so strong the first time to completely weak the second time? I could feel a definite difference."

She paused, looked down at her lap, and then up into my eyes, and said, "Remember when I told you, what you say to your mind you say to your body?"

"Yeah," I said, nodding.

"Well, the trick we just did shows exactly those words in action. Let me explain what I mean.

"When a thought goes through your mind, you react with

physical feelings in your body. So if your mind is filled with happy thoughts and pictures, like when you were having fun with your father, your body reacts to the happiness by feeling full of energy, strong and healthy. And . . ."

"And," I interrupted, "when I thought about my grandfather not talking to me over a dumb little thing like slamming the door on him, my body reacted with guilt, and that somehow I was bad.

"You know, Geula, I can even describe what it feels like in my body, sort of like a sinking in my stomach and this weak, nervous feeling all over. Just thinking about it now makes me feel terrible all over again."

Geula listened, then said, "It's amazing, isn't it, how much control your thoughts and feelings have over your body's reactions."

"You're right," I answered, nodding.

Carly pulled on Geula's skirt. "So what about my teeth? Wasn't this trick for my teeth?"

I shot her a look to be quiet, that this was my time.

Geula made a motion to me that it was all right, then reached out and touched Carly's hand.

"I'll tell you in a few minutes. Just listen now. Okay?" She took her hand off Carly's, turned back to face me, and asked, "Have you ever not wanted to go to school and talked yourself into a real stomachache? You've done it, haven't you, Mariel?"

"Yeah, lots of times," Mariel answered smiling, like it was no big deal telling the truth out loud.

I looked over toward Mariel, and smiled. "Yeah. Me, too," feeling not so bad about it, knowing that Mariel pulled the same stuff as me.

Geula looked from Mariel to me, then said, "Want me to tell you how you two talked yourself into getting sick?"

We both nodded, feeling a lot more curious than guilty.

Geula smiled, and began explaining. "Well, my guess is, you woke up wishing that you would get a stomachache so you wouldn't have to go to school, and the more you thought about it, picturing yourself sick and not going, the more real physical symptoms began to develop. Your mind said, 'I feel like I'm getting a stomachache,' so your digestive acids picked up the message and began to do their job on your empty stomach, making it hurt and cramp.

"Now with your stomach really hurting, your body began to tense up with the pain. The pain led to more tension, which made your stomach acids flow and your muscles tighten in reaction to the real pain, and now you were well on your way to a full-blown stomachache, and believed there was little you could do to stop it. And truly, at that moment, you probably couldn't. By this time you had so much real pain, you were sure your stomachache was all physical and that you had nothing to do with how it all began in the first place. Now you had your legitimate reason for not going to school, and none of it was your fault. Ah . . ." Geula waved her forefinger in the air, "but we know differently, don't we?"

Geula leaned forward. "I wouldn't feel too badly about it," she said, with a slight chuckle. "You're both really no different from anyone else. Most grown-ups do it on a daily basis and don't even know it. They don't seem to realize how much their thoughts and beliefs affect their health. Never mind the stresses they put themselves through every day."

I must have looked puzzled because she said, "Let me give you an example. Let's say someone sneezes in front of you, and you think, 'Cold germs, now I'm going to get a cold.' Chances are if you keep thinking about a cold and expecting to get it, no doubt you'll get one. After which, you'll probably say, 'See, I knew it was going to happen.' And maybe all the person had was dust in his nose."

"Maybe," I answered, half-listening, since Geula's words had stirred up thoughts of things that had been said to me that I worried about.

"Can I ask you a question, Geula? What you just said about believing about getting sick, is that the same as when my mother says that if I go out of the house with a wet head or without a scarf I'm going to get pneumonia?"

Geula nodded. "Exactly the same, if you believe it's true."

"I thought so. Well, I don't, that's why I sneak out and do it anyway, but I'm still afraid she's right and that one day because I didn't pay attention, I'll get pneumonia. And if I do, I know she'll either say, 'It serves you right for not listening to me,' or 'See, God punished you.' I wish she'd stop saying those things because it makes me think something bad really will happen to me."

"I'm sorry to disagree with what your mother tells you," Geula said, shaking her head, "but there's no way you're going to get pneumonia from a wet head or no scarf. Only bacteria can do that. But," she warned, "the more your mother holds the threat of sickness over your head, the more the fear will be in your mind, and the more likely it is you'll truly open yourself up for pneumonia.

"Now let me ask you a question. So with the cold and the pneumonia situations we just talked about, do you think you would get sick from the germs or from what you expect to happen?"

I shrugged. "The germs, right?"

Geula waved her forefinger at me. "Right, but only half-right.

"If you had a super-strong magnifying glass, and looked through it, you would see all kinds of germs and diseases floating around in the air. And did you know that the possibility for getting any of these diseases is already in your body, waiting for the right mental trigger?"

"That's hard to believe, Geula," I said.

"Well, believe it. It's true."

"You're saying if someone worries about a certain disease, like pneumonia, and believes and expects that they're going to get it, they could actually bring those germs and that illness into their body?"

Geula nodded. "Your mind is very powerful. What you expect, you get! And that means health as well as sickness.

"Did you ever notice some people are healthy most of the time, while others get sick a lot?

"Belief and expectation! That's the key!" Geula said, pointing her finger in the air.

I nodded. "I'm healthy most of the time, except for my bad sore throats. I get them a few times a year. They hurt so much I can hardly swallow."

Geula looked at me and paused for what seemed like a long time. "Maybe those are the stuck words you're afraid to say at home. Not being able to express yourself can be very painful."

Her words jolted me. I never thought of it that way. I'd be scared to death to talk to my parents so openly and honestly the way Mariel spoke to her. They wouldn't tolerate it. "Don't make waves or you'll be in trouble" was their motto.

"Geula," I asked, "since my stuck words are making me sick, do you think if I keep talking everything out with you instead of my parents, I won't get any more sore throats?"

Geula looked at me thoughtfully, then said, "It would be better if you could talk to them, but since it sounds like you can't, talking to me certainly would help get those stifled words and feelings out. And, by the way, being able to talk things out and look at symptoms would be a good idea for anybody who's reacting to or getting sick from upsetting thoughts."

She continued. "Your symptom, for example, is in your throat because you're afraid to express yourself. Somebody else might get it in a different place, like a headache or backache. Each person gets a symptom, or sometimes symptoms, in the very area that tells them what their minds are unhappy about.

"So if you get sick and want to feel better and be a healthy person, you need to listen to what your mind and body are telling you is going on inside your mind or feelings. And then do whatever it takes in order to become well."

Geula looked from Mariel to Carly to me. "Don't ever forget," she warned. "*You, and only you,* have control of your mind and body."

I looked back at Geula, wondering now about Carly's teeth.

"Geula," I asked, "If talking will cure my sore throats like you say, will talking and doing the 'God bless' exercises and thinking the right way make Carly's rotten teeth turn white and perfect?"

Carly's face brightened. "Will it?" she asked with hope in her voice.

Geula's eyes were moving from my face to Carly's and back.

"Oh, how I wish it were that simple," she said, shaking her head.

"As you know, Carly's baby teeth were damaged by the scarlet fever she had as an infant, and what your mother is doing, taking her to the dentist, is the only help she can get on those teeth."

I interrupted immediately. "Then why are we wasting our time doing the 'God bless' exercises for her teeth, if nothing will help?"

Instantly Geula's voice became sharp, "I never said nothing will help." Then it softened just as quickly. "What I said is that going to the dentist is the only help on her baby teeth. We're helping Carly work on her future teeth, her permanent ones. And we're not wasting our time with those.

"Every time you and Mariel and Carly and I say 'God bless' her teeth and think white perfect teeth, we are sending a message not only to 'God,' but to every cell in Carly's mind and body to believe and expect to grow perfect permanent teeth when she loses her baby teeth. And with the fluoride and calcium pills that the dentist is giving her now, everything is being done to make sure Carly is going to grow the best teeth possible."

Carly looked sadly up at Geula. "My baby teeth are going to stay rotten?"

Geula reached down and stroked Carly's dark curly hair lovingly. "I'm afraid so, Carly. But you can do something about your grown-up teeth. Put your energy into saying 'God bless my teeth' and think good thoughts about those pearly white, strong, healthy teeth that are growing in your gums right now. Okay? And I promise we're going to say 'God bless Carly's teeth' along with you until you get them."

Carly gave Geula the hugest grin as if her teeth were already beautiful and white.

Geula looked first at Mariel and then at me. "Right, girls?"

Mariel slightly nodded, and it was obvious from her sour expression that she was very irritated that the exercises took considerably longer than usual. It didn't seem to matter that she found out the cause of her fake stomachaches.

"Are we done yet?" she asked, glaring at her mother.

Geula patted Mariel gently on the shoulder. "I know you're bored, and I appreciate your patience. Thank you, honey."

I couldn't believe my ears. "Thank you?" A mother agreeing with a complaining child, and then thanking her? Unheard of in my family. I would have gotten "Who do you think you are, speaking that way to me?," followed by "And if you don't like it, lump it."

I was astonished at Geula's loving reaction to her daughter, and before I could control my surge of overwhelming feelings, "Geula, you're the best," fell out of my mouth.

Geula smiled, shocked by my compliment. "Why? What did I do that was so special?"

I smiled back, embarrassed by my uncontrolled display of emotion. "Never mind. You're just the best."

"Thank you," Geula answered slowly pulling herself up from the rug. We all took this as our signal to get up too.

"It's a beautiful sunny day. Why don't you find something to do outside?"

Mariel, still irritated by her mother's long talk, snapped back. "No, we're staying in. We're going to play on the porch." She tossed her head and stomped out the door. I followed passively behind, holding Carly by the hand.

Geula shrugged. "Suit yourself. Have fun."

I shook my head in amazement. Geula had to be somebody very special, to know this much and to act the way she did. Maybe one day very soon she would tell me. Maybe, if I was lucky, later today.

Purpose and Life lessons

Nothing was said as I had hoped and the day passed, and so did many days after that. Carly kept coming to the Franklins with me, and divided up her time between playing with Mariel and talking endlessly with Geula.

I could tell from the way Geula made sure to have daily talks with Carly that she believed there was definitely something special about her. But what?

My guess was that it had to do with the information Geula got that first day they met. I remember how strange Geula looked and acted. But since then, other than the added "God bless" exercises for Carly's rotten teeth, everything remained the same. Carly was treated no differently than Mariel and me. And because I didn't feel gypped or shortchanged in the attention department from Geula, I wasn't jealous of Carly at all. Which for me, was a feat since I wasn't too crazy about sharing anything, ever, with anyone, most especially Carly. And from the way Geula acted, Carly seemed to pose no threat to me, until that terrible day. . . .

We were about to play war with the lead soldiers. Carly and I were sitting on the floor watching Mariel, who sat cross-legged as she snapped open the metal latches and lifted the cover of the shiny white oil-cloth-covered carrying case. It was stuffed with all kinds of lead figures to be used for different wars.

There were Crusaders with horses, and lying next to them were American Revolutionary and British soldiers, and the blue and gray uniformed Civil War soldiers were scattered throughout.

But the largest assortment in the case were the World War II figures. There were men and women in khaki uniforms of all ranks, in fighting as well as standing positions. And a doctor and Red Cross nurses. Mariel even had a round mirror from an old pocketbook for a lake and a variety of trees and fences and trucks, which could be used in almost any game.

"Let's play World War II," Mariel said leaning over the suitcase while pulling out the khaki-colored figures. "Help me find all the right soldiers so we can play."

Carly and I sorted through the mishmash of figures and began piling them up on the concrete floor.

First we found the sergeants, then the WACS and WAVES, then the lieutenants, corporals, privates, and a general.

Mariel and I were busy putting wounded soldiers into the hospital tent to be attended by our Red Cross nurses, when Carly reached into the soldier pile and pulled out the general.

"I was the one who found the general doll," she said, holding him in her hand and stroking his head, "so I get to be the general."

I spun around and glared at her, but before I had a chance to open my mouth, Geula came rushing into the room. Her face was unusually serious. This was not the same person who had been calmly talking and smiling not more than half an hour ago. Instantly my stomach knotted. Maybe she knew I was just about to blast Carly and now I was going to get it.

Geula sat down in the peeling wrought iron armchair and leaned forward nervously, looking at Carly, Mariel, and me, but most particularly at me.

"There's something I need to talk to you about." She patted her chest. "I know it in here and it tells me to talk to you now and not to wait."

Her words scared me. The air on the porch was warm and humid, yet a chill shot through my whole body, causing huge goose bumps to break out all over my arms and legs. Even the hair on the back of my neck stood up on end.

I looked up at Geula, terrified by what she was about to say.

She looked down at the palms of her hands, then back up at me as though deciding something.

"Remember . . .," she paused, "Remember how I told you we can get information or help on our receivers from anywhere. . . ." Then she paused again. A long pause this time. She seemed uncomfortable talking, as if what she was going to say was difficult.

Personally, I was so relieved that nothing was going to happen to me, she could talk about anything, even something weird or horrible, and it would be okay.

Finally she spoke. "Well, I just got information from a long time ago . . . actually, centuries ago."

Geula hesitated and then began speaking again. "This may be hard for you to understand, but . . . remember how I stared at Carly and how excited I got when you brought her to my house?" She took a breath. "Well, I just found out Carly is more special than I even imagined."

My emotions went from relief, to curiosity, to shock. I sat motionless as my face fell.

Hard for me to understand? She got that right. And even harder to listen to.

I disguised my feelings by nodding and smiling like it really mattered, not wanting Geula to know that I was furious at her and jealous of Carly.

She must have been fooled by my act because she continued talking as if nothing was wrong.

"I knew immediately that there was something about her. But I had no idea what. So that first day when the two of you were standing there, I put out a question asking for information about her. And just now while I was in the kitchen cleaning up, a voice inside gave me information that Carly, in a past lifetime, had been a handmaiden in King Solomon's court."

Her words floored me as my competitive spirit flared.

Geula noticed my obviously shocked expression.

"I was surprised myself," she went on, "but as you know, I've come to accept and trust that all the messages and pictures that come to me are absolutely true. Even if they do seem unbelievable."

Geula's voice suddenly became more alive.

"Although I'm sure this is hard for you to believe, it is wonderful news, isn't it? Imagine! Your little sister!"

I sat there in silence. Wonderful? Geula had to be kidding. As usual, Carly was ruining everything for me. I knew I should've followed my instincts and done what I wanted to do in the first place, and that was leave her home. I shot a deadly look at Carly. She and Mariel were nonchalantly covering wounded soldiers with pieces of toilet paper, as if Geula had just announced the time instead of the shocker she had just delivered.

I glanced back at Geula, anger beginning to overwhelm me. How dare Geula say Carly was anything special, like a handmaiden to King Solomon, whatever that meant. I couldn't bear my sudden loss of status.

I took a deep breath to calm myself.

"What was I, Geula?" I asked coolly, but my insides were raging, begging her to tell me that I was someone important too. I was desperate to have the attention back on only me again and to be even more special than Carly.

Geula, sensing my anguish, didn't answer and instead stared into space as if waiting for an answer to my question to come from God or that universal information center that gave her the message about Carly.

Finally she turned her eyes back to me. "I don't know, Ivy," she said looking deeply at me. "Nothing's coming. I only know about Carly."

I could no longer disguise the anger and jealousy in my voice. I was livid that Carly was wrecking my special relationship with Geula, but at the same time, very interested to find out what information Geula had gotten about Carly.

"Well, what about her?" I said with obvious irritation in my voice. "I know who King Solomon is, but what's a handmaiden anyway?"

Geula reached over, put her fingers on top of mine, and looked at me compassionately. "Honey, I tried, but no information came about you. I'm sorry that you're so upset. None of us chooses the messages we get. They just come to us for whatever reason when they're supposed to. Right now, all I can tell you is the one I got about Carly, and what I think the message means. Is that okay with you?"

I nodded and swallowed hard, trying to keep the hurt and tears down. It was obvious that Geula wanted me to feel better, and I appreciated her caring, but at this moment it wasn't helping at all.

Geula leaned toward me and began speaking in a gentle voice. "When I said Carly was a handmaiden to King Solomon, what that meant was she was his closest personal servant. Back then a hand-maiden was chosen for this particular job because she was helpful and sensitive to whatever the king needed. She would listen to him talk and care about his feelings. And because she knew all of his secrets, she had to be someone he could trust."

I was about to interrupt, when Geula raised her hand to stop me. "Please, let me finish. Even though I didn't get information about you, I want you to know Carly isn't the only one who had special abilities in a past lifetime. You did too. And so did I, and so did Mariel. Everyone.

"Like I told you each person has a purpose for being here now. What I didn't tell you was that we've been carrying our special talents with us from one past lifetime to the next, right up to this moment."

Geula took a breath, then continued. "Those abilities that Carly had as a handmaiden back then are the same ones that you can already see in her now. Even though she's only three years old. But as she grows up her helpfulness and sensitivity will develop even more, so that she can use her special purpose with everyone she'll meet."

I looked back at Geula with a cynical expression.

"Geula, I can agree with the part about Carly being helpful and friendly, because it's true, she's already like that. But there's one thing you don't know about her. She can't be trusted with any-body's secrets. Carly's a blabbermouth," I said, happily tattling on her. "And I can't believe someone as smart as King Solomon ever trusted her. Her big problem is she always tells the truth and gets herself and me in trouble all the time with our parents. The reason I brought her here in the first place was more to keep her out of trouble with my mother and the Reilly kids than just to meet you. It was to protect her."

Geula looked shocked and shook her head in disbelief.

"Telling the truth is good, and Carly should be admired for doing it. But from what you're telling me, it sounds like maybe she's doing it too well."

Geula shook her head again, then said, "It looks to me that one of the life lessons Carly will have to work on and practice as she grows up, is to use her sensitivity to make better choices in what to say and how and when to say it."

"I sure hope she learns it fast," I said.

"I hope so too," Geula answered. She paused for a moment and added, "The good part for Carly and all of us is that we continuously get chances to learn, over and over again. Every day we're given experiences and people for us to test ourselves. Some to help us know we're doing well and to keep going, and others to help us look at where we still have things to learn.

"And hopefully, from all the opportunities we get, the good ones and the bad, we'll become the best we can be. At least, I know, we'll get the chance.

"Well," she said, suddenly cheerful, as she stood up. "I'll leave you all to discover whatever learning experience is in store for you. Hopefully it's a good one."

I glanced up at Geula. She returned my look and winked as I slid onto the porch floor to join Carly and Mariel with the hospital casualties. But suddenly my heart wasn't in the war game we were playing. For some unknown reason, I felt an incredible anxiety, from I didn't know where, overtake me.

And as the day passed, although everything appeared fine and we all were getting along better than ever, the uneasiness inside was rapidly growing. Something inside told me, loud and clear, that it was some kind of signal alerting me that some horrible thing was going to happen very soon, but for the life of me, I couldn't figure out what.

I looked over at Carly and Mariel, who were oblivious to my apprehension. Maybe the best thing for me to do would be to go home now and end the day. After all, there was tomorrow, and hopefully by then this terrible feeling would go away. Probably it was my fears and imagination working overtime, I rationalized, and I was making a big deal over nothing.

I reached over and touched Carly on the back.

"Come on," I said, "it's time to go home."

Carly turned to face me. "No. I don't want to go," she whined, tears beginning to well up in her eyes.

"If you leave nicely now, without a fuss, I promise you can come back with me tomorrow. Is it a deal?"

Carly's tears disappeared and were instantly replaced by a smile and a vehement nod.

"Help me clean up before we go," I said, grabbing for the carrying case. Carly and Mariel quickly pitched in, stuffing all the soldiers, trucks, and tents back into it.

I checked the floor to make sure we had gotten every figure. "See you tomorrow, Mariel, and tell your mother good-bye for me," I said, reaching for the porch door handle.

Carly took my free hand. "Tell your mother good-bye for me too," she mimicked.

I looked down at Carly and smiled at her as we left the porch. We walked along the Franklins' driveway and onto the tar-paved road for home.

Carly was chattering away about something, but my mind was so filled with other thoughts that I heard only her voice and not her words. I couldn't shake my dreadful doom, only now it was worse. Now it felt as if very soon something was about to take place that would end the relationship between Geula and me forever.

But would I be able to stop it before it happened?

I took a deep breath, shaking my head occasionally, going over all my mixed feelings as we walked. I should have listened to my first impulse and not brought Carly with me. She was definitely too young to come. And now I had to worry about her telling Mom and Dad everything that went on with Geula and Mariel. Carly and her big mouth. My luck that she had this life lesson to learn at my expense.

What I had to work on now was to speed up her learning and keep Carly from opening her mouth. Brainwash her. Manipulate her into silence. That's it.

I turned my attention to Carly and squeezed her hand lovingly. "Carly, honey," I began as sweetly as possible. "You liked going to Mariel's house today and playing with all the special toys and reading the comics, didn't you?"

Carly looked up at me with her round dark eyes. "Yes. I want to go tomorrow. You said I could. Right?"

"Yes. And you can go, but only on one condition. Otherwise, you'll have to stay home," I threatened pleasantly. "Are you listening?"

Carly nodded.

I stopped walking and squatted down face-to-face with Carly.

"You and I have to have a secret and not tell anybody, especially Mom and Dad. Do you understand?"

Carly nodded again.

I stared deeply into her eyes, and said, "Look at me and promise that you'll never, ever say anything about the 'God bless' exercises that we did with Geula and Mariel. And also, that you'll never say a word about that story that you were King Solomon's handmaiden. If Mom or Dad ask anything about what went on there, you can only say 'I played with toys and had a good time.'

Period. Nothing more. Let me hear what you're going to say," I pressed.

"I played with toys and had a good time," Carly repeated. "Is that right?"

"Yes. And you promise not to say anything else?"

Carly nodded. "I promise."

"Okay then, let's shake on it," I said, extending my hand.

Carly slid her little hand into mine and began shaking it hard, but even as we did, I knew all my talking and shaking hands was of no use. It was just a matter of time before our experiences at the Franklin house came out. I knew Carly couldn't stop herself, even if she wanted to. After all, it wasn't her fault that she was only a little kid and a talkative and truthful one at that. Also she had this lesson to learn.

I would just have to pray and wait.

The Unavoidable

As much as I tried to convince myself that everything would be all right, the feeling of doom never went away. I knew that time with the Franklins was precious, so each day, rain or shine, I was up by eight o'clock making sure to get in as much time with them as possible. I continued to bring Carly with me so she wouldn't be able to blab to our mother when I wasn't at home to stop her. Besides, I wouldn't have had the heart to leave her anyway, especially when she looked at me with her guilt-producing, tear-filled puppy dog eyes.

Each morning, I helped Carly get dressed, fed her the usual bowl of corn flakes, and locked the front door quietly behind us as we walked hand in hand down the familiar road to the Franklin house.

These days, something told me that it was necessary to spend all my time with Geula, and to leave the playing with Mariel to Carly, who was more than happy to fill in my former spot. And when I was with Geula, I took in every idea and every sentence, repeating her words over and over to make sure I would remember as much of her teachings as possible.

It didn't even matter that I didn't exactly understand everything Geula talked about, as long as I sort of got the gist of it and memorized most of her words. I figured that as I got older, the meaning eventually would make sense to me.

And when I became anxious and told Geula that I wasn't able to understand something she was saying, she would explain it again in even more detail. And when I still didn't totally get it, she would smile gently and say, "Honey, don't worry so much. I promise, one day, when the timing is right, everything I've been teaching you will become crystal clear."

I nodded and continued to ask more and more questions, knowing in my heart of hearts that time was running out fast.

And was I ever right! What I was afraid would happen, happened.

It took place on the one day that I couldn't resist playing "Queens County Savings Bank" in Mariel's father's desk.

Mariel and I had divided the play money from the Monopoly game between us and were busy using the date stamper and ink pad as we added new dates and numbers to some old canceled bankbooks we had found. Carly was in the kitchen watching Geula peel potatoes for the French fries we were going to have for lunch. She wasn't particularly interested in our game and loved the special attention Geula lavished on her each time she visited. It was hard to say whether Carly came to the Franklins' house for the toys and comic books or for Geula's love. Either way, I didn't feel as jealous as the first time they met and surprisingly felt good that she was finally getting everything she needed from a mother.

The desk Mariel and I were playing on was within earshot of the kitchen and I could hear Carly's high-pitched voice coming though the open doorway. For some unknown reason, something inside told me it was a good idea for me to eavesdrop on the conversation she was having with Geula.

Being an expert at doing two things at once, I arranged the play money into a shoebox in stacks of ones, fives, tens, twenties, fifties, and hundreds, while I strained my ears to hear what Carly and Geula were talking about.

"Mommy grabbed me by my hair and yanked it really hard," I could hear Carly say. "It really hurt a lot, and when I started to cry, Mommy said, 'So I pulled your hair. Don't make such a big deal out of it. Pulling your hair will make it grow stronger.'

"Geula, do you think my hair is growing stronger?" I heard Carly ask.

The only response from Geula was the word "No," and nothing else. Dead silence.

My heart sank. For me, because I knew something was said that couldn't be taken back, and for my family because it was embarrassing that an outsider knew about our mother's behavior.

Whenever Mom got into a temper and pinched our faces or pulled our hair, she would never admit she was wrong for doing it or apologize. Instead she would try to fluff off the incident by making it seem as if what she had done was really for our own good, like giving us rosy cheeks or strong hair. Maybe she convinced herself with this nonsense, but she never fooled me. And I had avoided her angry outbursts at all costs for as long as I could remember. But not poor Carly.

And now she had finally gone and done it. Been too truthful. One of our family secrets was out in the open, and told to Geula, of all people. It was obvious Carly wasn't trying to get our mother in trouble. She was just innocently talking as if this was a normal family occurrence and that it happened in every family. Little did she know.

I continued going through the motions of calmly playing bank teller with Mariel, but my mind and ears were in the kitchen with Geula and Carly. My stomach was in knots and I felt like throwing up as I strained to pick up any little bit of the conversation drifting through the doorway.

All I could hear was Carly happily chattering away, and sounds like "ums" and "uh-huhs" coming out of Geula. She wasn't talking in her usual animated and verbal way, and my body suddenly became frozen with fear and knowing. Something terrible was going to happen. Everything inside me was screaming that message, loud and clear. It was just a matter of time. But, what exactly, I couldn't figure out.

I sat glued to the chair by the desk, afraid to get up and embarrassed to actually go into the kitchen. The minutes seemed like hours as I went through my charade with Mariel and waited for Geula to make the first move. Finally she called us into the kitchen for our French fry lunch. I tried to listen for something in her tone that might tell me what was going on inside of her, but her voice gave nothing away.

At her call, I anxiously jumped up out of the chair without waiting for a second time, ran into the kitchen, and sat down next to Carly, who was contentedly chewing on a French fry. Mariel parked herself on the empty chair on Carly's other side, grabbed for one of the fries, and popped it into her mouth.

I had no appetite and my only concern was to carefully watch Geula as she moved silently around the kitchen. First she put the ketchup down on the table, then three glasses of milk, one for each of us. All without one word. It was obvious from the frown on her face that she was beyond extremely upset. Never had I seen her look like this.

Carly and Mariel were unaware of her mood and were busy

talking and dipping French fries in little puddles of ketchup. I sat like a lump, not having the energy or heart to join them. My throat was so constricted that I could hardly swallow, and I managed to go through the motions of eating by nibbling on a few French fries and taking a couple sips of milk. And all the while I never took my eyes off Geula as she quietly moved about the kitchen.

Usually she pulled up a chair and ate or drank something with us. But today, nothing.

Finally she glanced over at us. "Are you finished?" she asked, with an edge to her voice. And without waiting for an answer, she began clearing the dishes and glasses off the table and immediately brought a plate of oatmeal cookies for us.

"Girls, there won't be any 'God bless' exercises today," Geula announced in an unusually authoritative voice as she handed the cookies to Mariel. "Here. Take this plate and go out on the porch and play." Startled by her tone, Mariel looked at her mother's face, and without a word, obediently got off her chair. She took the plate from Geula and walked quickly toward the door. I stood up, helped Carly off her chair, took her by the hand, and rapidly followed.

My heart was pounding out of control as my fear took over. In all the times I had been coming to the Franklins, not once had we skipped "God bless" exercises. And I knew better than to ask Geula why we weren't going to do the exercises and what was going to happen instead. There was nothing to do but keep my mouth shut and wait for Geula to make the next move.

I sat on the peeling wrought iron armchair near the French doors that separated the porch from the dining room so that I could keep my eye on Geula. Carly and Mariel were quietly putting the marbles into the holes on the Chinese checkers board, but I was too busy watching Geula through the lace-curtained open door to care much about anything except her mood. I could see her pacing back and forth across the room, shaking her head "no" from time to time.

This had to be the worst and longest day of my life as I watched and waited helplessly for something to happen. I looked up at the clock over the glider. Four o'clock. It definitely would be a good idea to go home early, I decided, wanting to make a quick getaway from the mounting tension. Better yet, we would skip tomorrow and come the day after. And maybe if I took Carly out of Geula's sight for a while, she would forget what Carly had told her today and things would return to normal by the time we came back.

I quickly stood up. "Mariel, we have to go home early today," I lied. "Right, Carly?" I nodded vehemently and gave Carly one of my father's "you'll get killed if you don't agree" looks. Carly knew I meant business and nodded back to me.

"Then hurry up, let's go," I said, trying to act as if we had to leave for a very important reason. "If you're good, I'll play with you at home." I smiled in a friendly way for Mariel's benefit. Lucky for me, and for whatever reason, whether Carly wasn't in the mood to be argumentative or really wanted to go home and play, she got up off the porch floor and took my hand.

"See you tomorrow, Mariel," I lied again, and crossed the fingers of my free hand behind my back.

Carly smiled and waved good-bye. "See you tomorrow," she repeated, copying me.

As the porch door slammed behind us, I looked down at her with a mixture of anger and pity. Poor dumb little kid. She had no idea the trouble her habit of telling too much of the truth had caused us today.

My only hope was that it would all blow over by the time we returned to the Franklins. But would it? Or was it too late?

THE PAIN OF A PROBLEM

When Carly woke up the next morning and asked about going to the Franklins, I reminded her that we weren't going today because we had planned a special play date. Just for the two of us, and no one else. Not that I had any interest in it. For me the day was going to be torture, but our playing together seemed to please Carly as much as going to the Franklins. Thank goodness.

I pulled out the coloring books, dumped the crayons on the floor, and let Carly do whatever she wanted, just to keep her happy, and most of all, quiet. I had no head for trouble today since my stomach was still a mess even after a whole night's sleep. I couldn't get Geula's distraught face and her pacing back and forth out of my mind.

It was ten o'clock. Mom had just gotten out of bed and was having her usual cup of coffee in the kitchen when the doorbell rang.

Who would be here this early in the morning? Maybe it was the mailman with some kind of special delivery letter since the milkman already came earlier.

I jumped up from my seat on the floor and ran down the hall to the window in the spare room that overlooked our front stoop to see who it was. But no matter how much I craned my neck, I couldn't make out the person standing there.

Then I heard the voice. My breath caught in my throat and my body froze in its tracks.

It was Geula. How did she find out where we lived? I racked my brain. Did I tell her and hadn't remembered?

No. I was careful to protect myself.

My heart was pounding so hard, I could feel it practically coming through my skin. It was obvious why she was here. And it wasn't just a social visit. It was about Carly and her big mouth.

I knew Geula was upset by what Carly had told her, but I never figured she would show up on our doorstep. No doubt her desire to help people with problems was so strong, she probably believed talking with Mom would teach her how to be a better mother and then everything would be happier for all of us. No way. She had to be kidding thinking any talk with Mom would change a thing.

I motioned for Carly to be quiet as we stationed ourselves at our usual listening post at the top of the upstairs landing. We couldn't be seen by anybody downstairs in the living room below, but we could hear every word fairly well.

Pushing my head hard up against the round wooden balustrades, I strained to hear as much of the conversation as possible.

"Your children have been coming to my house to play with my daughter, Mariel. And what lovely children they are," I heard Geula say in her gentle, warm tone of voice to our mother. "By the way, I'm your neighbor from down the block, Geula Franklin. So nice to meet you."

"It's nice to meet you too," Mom answered pleasantly, surprisingly nice for her, considering morning was not her best time. "Come in and sit down," she said.

From the direction of their voices, it was obvious that they were sitting opposite each other on the green down-filled-cushioned armchairs next to the fireplace.

"Did you just come to socialize, or was there a problem with the children?" Mom asked Geula.

There was a long pause from Geula. "Well both, actually," she said hesitantly. And then it all came out, the real reason Geula was here, and it wasn't just to chitchat—just as I had suspected.

"I came here because I wanted very much to meet you, but also to tell you about something that I heard yesterday from Carly that disturbed me very much."

Our mother snickered. "Oh that Carly, always making up stories. What did she say this time that you would possibly take so seriously?"

Mom was already dismissing what Carly had said as worthless without even hearing it, and no doubt expected Geula to do the same. But Geula went on.

"Oh, you should take her seriously," Geula said, sounding surprised by Mom's reaction. "Your Carly is a very special child. I knew that the minute I laid eyes on her.

"Your children and my daughter and I have been calling on God's help to give Carly healthy new teeth, and that's when I found out all about her. Her past, that is.

"It happened one day while I was cleaning up in the kitchen. This information came to me, that in a previous lifetime, Carly had been a handmaiden in King Solomon's court. I know it's hard to believe. Your Carly." Then Geula added, "But, now that you know, you can better understand why she is the way she is. Even at three, she's already showing her handmaiden ways."

I was horrified by Geula's honesty and waited for Mom to respond. But surprisingly she said nothing. Probably she was too much in shock over what Geula was saying.

Geula, however, must have taken Mom's silence as a signal to go on.

"Like I told you," she continued, "I also have a young daughter, and from my experiences with her, I know just how difficult even the best of children can be. With all their trying behavior, it's very hard for a mother to be patient. And especially with two children to look after, like you have."

Then Geula's voice took on a tone of deep concern for Mom.

"But, no matter how impossible they can be, and how frustrated you feel, I've learned it works so much better to talk nicely to them and not let your anger get the best of you. Physically disciplining them isn't good for any of you."

For a moment there was a long, dead silence. Then Mom spoke.

"What are you talking about?" I could hear the rage growing in her voice. "What exactly did Carly tell you?"

Every cell in my body froze in terror. Knowing Mom and her over-reacting, this meeting wasn't going to end well either for Geula or for Carly and me.

Geula went on and repeated the hair-pulling story. And then she ended by saying, "Carly is such a bright little girl, with such an independent mind of her own. You know what I've learned by raising Mariel? Children have exactly the same feelings as we do. It's just that their bodies are smaller. I found out that what they need and want from us as parents is loving guidance. And with a child like Carly, if you want her to mind you, just listen to her and teach her in a kind way. With her, force doesn't work. I know, having spent time with her."

There was an even longer silence than before. Neither Geula nor Mom said anything. I was dying to see what was going on in the room, their expressions or how they were sitting, but all I could do was wait in a panic for someone to break the deadly silence.

Mom must have been horrified that Carly had told on her. And worse yet, embarrassed that Geula was giving her lessons on how to be a good mother. Neither one was going to sit well with her, that I knew for sure.

Then Mom erupted.

"Who do you think you are coming here and telling me how to raise my children?" she shrieked. "King Solomon's handmaiden, indeed. You're as big a liar as Carly is. What nerve you have!"

Mom stormed to the door and pulled it open so furiously that it crashed back into the wall with a loud thud.

"Get out of here and take your insane ideas with you, you crazy woman." Mom was still yelling at the top of her lungs. "Go raise your own child and I'll take care of mine."

And no doubt, she was going to "take care" of us now, but good.

The door slammed closed.

"You two, come down here. Right now," Mom ordered in a rage.

My entire body shook with terror and there was a look of panic on Carly's face. We both stood up quickly, knowing better than not to do what she wanted immediately, even if she killed us. I ran down the stairs with Carly close behind me, all the while praying we weren't going to get more than just screamed at. Because with Mom there was no way of ever knowing how she was going to react.

I stood in front of her while she shook her finger in my face. Carly hid slightly behind me, hoping to disappear. The only thing

I could make disappear was my mind. All I could think about was running away, while Mom continued ranting at us.

"You'll be sorry you ever opened your mouth," she yelled. "And that crazy woman. She's a danger. She should be put away. Children shouldn't be allowed to go near her with her ridiculous ideas. And what does an old woman of her age know about raising children, anyway? Listen to children and talk kindly to them as if they're little adults," she sneered. "Did you ever hear of such insanity?"

Mom moved forward, right on top of me and glared into my eyes. I stiffened in fear.

"And you. I thought you had more sense than to listen to a woman like her. And how dare you bring Carly there? Where are your brains?"

Then she turned her attention to Carly, who by now was hiding completely behind me for protection.

Her voice was a mixture of anger and ridicule. "You, King Solomon's handmaiden, indeed. That's a laugh."

Carly and I stood immobilized, hoping her temper would run its course and that she would calm down a little.

Finally, she pointed to the staircase. "Go to your room and stay there until I tell you to come out. Just wait until your father comes home and hears about what happened. You'll be sorry you were born. This is only the beginning. Mark my words."

Carly and I didn't need to be told a second time. We ran upstairs and disappeared into our room to stay out of her sight. Maybe if we were lucky she would have time to cool off. And hopefully after a while, take what Geula had said not so seriously. But even as I thought it, I knew it was only wishful thinking.

Carly and I spent the day mostly in silence, both of us afraid of Mom's threat and the unknown horrible punishment when Dad came home.

When we heard his voice downstairs, neither Carly nor I ran down to say hello as we usually did. Instead we sat looking at each other fearfully and waited in dread of what was going to happen to us. I knew that Mom was going to tell him everything the minute he walked in the door.

No big surprise. I was right.

Through our closed bedroom door, I could hear his raised voice and the heaviness of his shoes as he stomped up the stairs.

The door to our bedroom was flung open. His gray eyes had that wide, icy look as he grimly walked to the center of our room.

Carly and I instantly slid off our beds and stood silently at attention, facing him as he stared down intimidatingly at us. I was too terrified and also knew better than do anything when he got this angry.

"You two," he began with cold authority. "I don't want either of you around that sick woman ever again. Do you understand me?" he said, glaring at us. "And if I or your mother catch either of you going to that house again, you'll be severely punished. Do I make myself clear?"

Carly and I nodded our heads like puppets, not daring to move more than our necks in case his anger changed to rage.

And without another word, he turned around and walked back downstairs. I sank to my knees, took a deep breath, and thanked God that it wasn't worse.

I couldn't believe how furious he was and it wasn't even about him. But I knew that no matter what, they always stuck together in the anger-and-punishment department.

However, today, they were both "off-the-wall" over Geula's visit. Personally, I was more upset with Carly for telling Geula about the hair pulling, which was the cause of all the trouble. But I knew she couldn't keep secrets when I brought her there in the first place and really had only myself to blame for the mess. After all, she was only three years old. How could I expect a little kid to know or even understand our unspoken family agreement, which was: Whatever goes on in our house, stays in our house, even if it's horrible or wrong. You never tell anyone. You don't even admit it to yourself. You just wait until the problem goes away and then everything will be back to normal again.

Only this time, I knew, with everything in me, that it wasn't going to go away. Ever. Our parents were adamant about our never seeing Geula again, and attempting to question or trying to talk to them about how kind and smart she really was would be useless. Neither one was good at listening to reason from anyone, most especially from their children.

There was no choice but to recognize and accept the reality.

It was all over.

My relationship with Geula was finished, for good.

MESSAGES AND GUIDES

Or was it?

Good thing I never acted on the decisions that I made at night. Usually at night in bed, I pictured the worst-case scenarios. Lying there, I would imagine all kinds of failures and talk myself into feeling helpless and that nothing I really wanted could possibly work out. But the minute it was daylight, for some unknown reason, I felt better. More in control of my life again. Hopeful thoughts would begin to fill my mind and I had better perspective on whatever my problems were.

Morning was best for me because when the house was quiet I could lie in my bed staring up at the ceiling, and let thoughts drift in and out of my mind while I sorted out my life. Some of my best creative ideas and answers came to me that way. And this morning I needed plenty.

A moan from Carly disrupted my daydreaming. I rolled over and glanced to see if she was waking up, but fortunately, she was still asleep. This morning, more than ever, I didn't have the patience to listen to her babble and needed time to think.

I positioned myself on my back again and closed my eyes to work on my problem of not being allowed to see Geula, when out of nowhere, an image of the game I used to play in the Bronx with the books from my parents' bookcase popped into my mind.

A sign! I quickly pulled back the top sheet and got out of bed. I tiptoed over to the bookcase to survey all the books lined up on the three shelves. What does the sign want me to read? Staring into the maze of books, I sat waiting for some answer to come inside. Finally, something urged me to pull out my Famous People's book. And as I held it in my lap, that same inner feeling guided my hand to open it to the page that was obviously there for me to see.

I couldn't believe who was staring back from the page.

Walt Disney.

This sign had to be a message from God or that information giver that Geula had talked so much about. Suddenly, something she had taught me flashed into my mind. "Special people, like Walt Disney, never give up, no matter what happens or what anyone says. You must always say 'Yes' to the ups and downs of life." Then as I sat there thinking of Geula, a familiar expression of my grandfather's also appeared. "Where there's a will, there's a way," he would say.

Without a doubt, these two messages pieced together had to be my answer, and it didn't take much thinking to figure out what to do.

This was one of those downs of life and the message meant not to give up, no matter what my mother and father said. They weren't going to deprive me of seeing Geula, regardless of the consequences. I had the will, and I was going to find the way.

But how was I going to manage visiting Geula without anyone knowing where I was? Meaning my parents.

My mother had warned me many times that she "had eyes in

the back of her head" and that she could watch me even when she wasn't there. I didn't really believe her, but I was still nervous about the idea that maybe it was possible.

My watch on the night table read eight o'clock. If I was going to do it, the only time would be now. Dad had already left for work and Mom and Carly were still sleeping. I could easily sneak out of the house without either of them knowing where I was going.

I reached down for my blue shorts and white T-shirt that were laying on the floor from yesterday. Last night I had thrown off my clothes, not caring if I lived or died, but with the sign today, it was a different story. I picked up my moccasins and carried them in my hand while tiptoeing out of the bedroom and down the stairs. I quietly closed the front door behind me.

So far, so good.

Breathing a sigh of relief at my successful getaway, I dropped the moccasins on the front path, slid my feet into them, and began to walk the road to Geula's house.

To cover myself when Mom gave me the third degree about where I went, I decided that my alibi would be to tell her I was sitting by the brook. After all, neither she nor my father said anything about not going there.

Even though the wild blackberries to prove where I was were all gone, if I came home with a lovely bouquet of Queen Anne's Lace and Black-eyed Susans for Mom after my secret visit with Geula, she'd definitely believe me. And hopefully be happy with my peace offering too.

Besides being at the brook wouldn't be a complete lie because I could go into Geula's backyard through the path from the woods and then back home the same way.

At the sight of the field, I left the road, hiked through it, now overgrown with early fall's goldenrod and red-tipped sumac flowerets, and moved into the cool of the tall oak forest. I stepped carefully on the slimy moss-covered rocks that poked out of the rushing water and crossed the brook to the other side and the path that would take me into Geula's backyard.

The path was much shorter than I had remembered and I found myself in her backyard almost immediately.

Running through her yard in case my mother's eyes in the back of her head could possibly see me, I entered the porch and knocked on the lace-curtained French doors.

Suddenly, for some reason, my whole body tensed up and my heart began racing. Was it because of my sneaking here and my fear of getting in trouble, or was it a signal that something else even worse was going to happen?

I took a deep breath to calm my nerves and peeked through the lace curtain and saw Geula coming across the room. The door opened. The sight of her was too much for me as I began to cry and talk at the same time.

"I'm so sorry, Geula, for what happened yesterday. I never wanted you to get in trouble. You meant well but my mother didn't want to listen. And last night my father laid down the law and said that Carly and I could never come here again and see you. But this morning I got a sign and had to come. I hope you don't get into any more trouble because of me."

Geula reached out and put her hand reassuringly on my shoulder. At her touch I took a breath and tried to relax myself a little although my body was still shaking.

"Don't worry, I can take care of myself," she said gently. "And you don't have to apologize either. What happened wasn't your fault or Carly's in any way.

"I knew you got a sign and that you would be here early this morning, that's why I've been up waiting for you. Mariel's still asleep and you and I need this time now for ourselves, so I'm not going to wake her." Then Geula paused and looked straight into my eyes.

"Come, let's sit down so we can talk."

Every hair on my body stood on end as Geula spoke. This time I didn't have to ask where she got her information. I already understood.

Geula offered her hand and led me into the house and out to her sunroom. She motioned for me to sit on one of the white-painted rattan chairs and made herself comfortable on the one facing me. A ball of anxiety knotted in my stomach as I waited for her to talk.

We continued to look at each other in silence for what seemed an eternity. Finally she leaned forward and touched my arm, not lovingly though, more with an urgency that I felt throughout my whole body.

"I already know what happened at your house last night," she began, "and I'm so sorry you had to go through such misery."

A pain began to rise in my chest. "You never should have come to my house, Geula."

"I had to, honey. You know I had no choice," Geula answered softly. "Someone has to help make changes in people's lives, otherwise the world will go on the same old way. People continuing to be afraid and angry. People controlling and hurting each other. And hardest to understand of all, those they're supposed to care about and love.

"I know your mother believes she's a good parent. However, some of her ways are hurtful. I wanted to help, but sadly she took it the wrong way and got embarrassed by what she had done to Carly and felt threatened by what I was saying. That's why she yelled. Her anger was a cover-up for her fear and shame."

"I'm sorry she was so mean to you," I stammered.

"I know you are," Geula said, putting up her hand to stop me from continuing. "But your mother is no different than many other good people who act mean when they're faced with someone who looks or thinks in ways they don't understand. They take any new idea or belief as a personal threat to be challenged and stopped immediately."

Geula hesitated for a moment, then went on.

"There's something I must tell you now," she said, staring straight into my eyes. "So listen carefully."

My body tensed at her words.

"Remember when you asked me if people think I'm strange?"

I nodded, remaining silent.

"The answer is yes." Geula sighed deeply. "Unfortunately. Many people have been uncomfortable and threatened by me and my ideas. Some have made fun of me; others, like your parents, have tried to get rid of me.

"But I'm used to it, because as I've told you already, what I believe and teach is my whole life. It's the reason I'm here on this earth. So no matter what anyone says or does to me, I have to continue to do what I'm here for. And whatever will happen to me, I can't allow another's fear or threats to stop me from believing in myself and helping others in the world.

"And neither can you. I want you to remember that always." She leaned forward and stared deeply into my eyes.

"Will you promise me that?"

I nodded again.

"Good," Geula said, seeming satisfied, then suddenly her expression became somber. She reached over and placed her hand on top of mine. "You and I both know this is the last time we're going to be together."

I was stunned, hearing her words. "No," I protested, my eyes filling with tears. "Don't say that. It's not true."

I jumped up from the chair and put my arms around her neck. "I love you so much, Geula. You have to be here with me forever."

Geula put her smooth strong arms around me and held me close while I began sobbing uncontrollably. My nose filled with her lavender scent, and that familiar smell made my body ache even more.

"Shhh . . .," she said, trying to comfort me. "I will be here with you, forever, just not physically like this. Listen carefully and I'll tell you how we'll do it."

I stopped crying, confused by her words, and looked up into her face.

"What do you mean?"

Geula put her forefinger to her mouth to silence me.

"Just believe and follow everything I'm about to tell you even if you don't completely understand.

"Will you do as I ask?"

I nodded, desperate for any chance to be with her.

"Okay. Then, go sit in your chair so I can show you how whenever you just want to be with me or maybe when you need some answer, you'll be able to see me and hear me, almost like we are right now."

I sat back into my chair and stared blankly at Geula.

"How will I be able to see you if I'm not with you, Geula?" I asked, still not grasping it.

She put up her hand to stop me. "You will. Please, hear me out."

"Now," she began explaining, "have you ever thought about someone you missed and then some memory of them instantly popped into your mind?"

I nodded. "As you said that, I just remembered playing on my back porch in the Bronx with my friends, Alan and Edwin."

"And all you had to do was remember them in your mind and there they were. Right?"

"Yeah," I said, suddenly understanding. "Let me see if I got it. When we see people in our memory, that's the way we keep them alive with us forever. Is that it?"

Geula smiled. "In a sense, yes. But not just people. Every book or movie you ever loved, each happy time you enjoyed or problem you faced are all stored up inside of you like a library. All you have to do is think about something or someone, and there they are, real as life back in your memory, ready for your use."

At this last statement, I frowned, not quite grasping this "use" part. "What use? How?" I asked.

Geula replied quickly, "For your enjoyment, but mostly to get experiences and answers. I'll show you in a moment."

She paused a moment, and said, "I don't know whether you realize it, but there are lots of people out there for your use, more than you can imagine."

"Like who?" I questioned.

"Well," Geula went on, "first, there are those people who will be in your life for a very long time, like your mother and father and Carly. You get most of your experiences from them."

"Yeah, but not always good ones," I interjected, still remembering how today's painful meeting came about in the first place.

"That's true," Geula replied. "However, for you to grow into the person you're meant to be, you need everything, both the good times and the hard ones. Remember how I taught you about that?"

I stared at her numbly but said nothing.

"And then there are those people you meet for only a few minutes, like maybe someone you might talk to on a train."

"Or some kid in the doctor's office," I added.

"Exactly," Geula said, then looked into my eyes.

"Now this may be a little harder to understand. There are also those people whom you've never even met, but for some unknown reason are sending you messages on your information receivers. Some might be from the future, who maybe one day you'll actually get to meet. And then there are others. Ones from the past. Like an old relative who died that you think about, or those friends from the Bronx you just mentioned that you don't see anymore, but care about and miss.

"Or," Geula paused, "someone from way, way in the past, maybe from centuries ago."

"Like the one who gave you the information about Carly being King Solomon's handmaiden," I said.

Geula raised an eyebrow and smiled. "Could be."

Then her smile faded. "And one more group," she said softly. "Those like me, who will be with you for only a short time and then that time will be over."

The sickening pain immediately returned in full force, and before either of us had a chance to feel too much, she went on.

"But don't worry," Geula said slowly, leaning forward to reinforce her words. "Like all the others I just mentioned, I will be there to help you whenever and wherever you need."

She put her hand on my hand reassuringly. "Always. I promise."

"But how will you be there for me?" I asked, more desperate than ever. "And how will the others you just talked about be able to help me?"

Geula listened intently, then replied. "Remember, when I wanted information about Carly?"

I stared at her but said nothing.

"Well, when I need answers or help, I ask my question, and then wait to see who or what comes to me.

"Sometimes," she went on, "I can actually see who it is very clearly. It can be someone familiar or not. But at other times, I don't see anyone. I have no idea who's giving me what I need. It might be God, or any of the other people from who knows where sending me the information that I pick up on my receivers, either by hearing or feeling it, or just knowing it for sure inside. Sometimes, I even get messages and signs that pop up out of nowhere, like from talking to someone that I hadn't expected to meet.

"We're constantly being sent guidance. All we have to do is tune into the messages around us, and learn to interpret the information to help us make the decisions we need to make."

Geula looked at me intensely, then added, "And it's really easy, too. Just have complete faith and know that if you keep quiet and don't try to control what's happening, the direction and what you need will absolutely be there."

A surge of impatience welled up in me at how casually she was taking her life, and now mine.

"Maybe so, Geula," I said, with an edge to my voice. "But what if I'm waiting for signs and nothing happens? Am I just supposed to sit there like a dummy? I have to do something. Then I can figure out my own solutions. Right?"

"Oh sure, if you want to get in the way of the real answers."

Geula persisted. "Let's go back to the information about Carly. When I first saw her, a sudden feeling told me there was something very special about her. Now most people, when they get those gut feelings, usually ignore them or rationalize them away with some logical thought like, 'Don't be ridiculous, she's just an ordinary, nice, little child. Stop making more of this.'

"But you see, I know better. I couldn't let it go. I know from experience that my gut feelings never lie and were telling me something very important. My rationalizing mind may lead me down the wrong path, but never my feelings. And since I've come to trust them completely, I asked the universe for help on who she was. And maybe from God or one of the spirits or people from the past, the information flashed into my mind telling me who."

"Didn't you ever think you were making it up or the answer you got was crazy?"

Geula shook her head vehemently. "I absolutely knew I wasn't making it up. And yes, some people might have thought it was crazy, but I know better.

"When I get information, no matter how wild or way out it may seem, I trust it with all the blind faith in me to take it as truth and the very answer I need. I never, never doubt or don't listen and think I know better, because when I do, that's when I'm most wrong.

"I've learned over many, many years of making mistakes," Geula said, looking directly at me, "to watch out for my negative, controlling ways and to stick with my gut and my heart and keep an open mind. Because then, and only then, will I get the right answers."

Suddenly Geula's face grew solemn.

"Much as I hate to say it, our time together is running out. Soon Mariel will be up and you'll have to go, but before you do, it's very important that I show you how to get that help I was talking about.

"Especially when you want it from me," she said, touching my arm for emphasis.

My face grew pale at her words.

"It's going to be okay," Geula said, sensing my pain. "Believe me, I'm not any happier than you, but you'll see once we get going, you'll begin to feel a whole lot better."

I nodded, half-heartedly. "How do I start?"

Geula said nothing for a few minutes, then asked, "Remember how we did our 'God bless' exercises?"

I nodded again.

"All right, then," she continued, with a tone of urgency in her voice, "tell me in detail everything you can recall."

I looked up nervously at Geula as I recited our daily ritual.

"First we get into a comfortable position," I began remembering. "Then we close our eyes, and take a deep breath in and hold it, then slowly let the air out. We do that again a few more times, while you tell us to relax our face and neck and chest and stomach. Every part of our bodies, right down to our feet. And we keep breathing and relaxing, more and more, until it's like we're half asleep. Then we do the 'God bless' part."

Geula nodded the whole while I talked. "That's right," she said, "and now we're going to do the same relaxing part, only this time instead of continuing with the 'God bless' portion of the exercise, I'm going to guide you into something different.

"Listen carefully. This time, instead, what I want you to do is let yourself hear, see, smell, taste, feel, and know everything that comes to you. Just let it come into your mind and body. I don't want you to question or think about whether it's real or not. Just accept whatever comes in as real. Trust and believe everything. Do you understand me?"

I gave her a puzzled look.

Geula leaned toward me.

"This may be difficult for you," she said, weighing each word, "but go along with me. It's very important that you do." And then added, "And stay alert for the messages."

The power of her tone startled me and as I looked into her face, her expression gave me goose bumps all over—my signal that something extraordinary was happening or going to.

"Let's begin," she said, her voice suddenly softening. "Get really comfortable, with your feet flat on the floor."

I took off my moccasins, moved around on the chair until I was satisfied with my position, and placed my hands palms down on my knees.

"Ready now?" Geula didn't wait for my answer and began speaking in a quiet monotone, yet directive voice. "Okay then, allow your eyes to close gently and begin to let go of anything in your mind . . . let go and relax. Now, focus on your breathing. Allow your breathing to be comfortable . . . deep and even . . . Inhale and feel the air filling out your lungs . . . let your chest expand . . . hold it . . . and as you slowly breathe out let your chest go loose . . . feel your whole body relaxing."

I followed Geula's instructions, and as expected from the "God bless" exercises, I felt my arms getting heavy and a tingly sensation developing in my fingertips.

Geula had said the first time we did the exercises that this was my body relaxing. She also said I could get up at any time and that I wasn't in any danger of doing something I didn't want to do, so I wasn't nervous about the weird changes in my body.

Geula's voice remained soft and steady. "And as you continue to breathe deeply, let all your muscles relax, your face, your neck . . . loose and relaxed . . . your shoulders, your chest, arms . . . let your breathing be deep and even . . . relax your stomach, your legs. . . . Feel your whole body relax deeper and deeper into the chair. Let yourself be open as you let go and relax. As you continue to focus on your breathing, feel the air filling every cell, making you feel lighter and lighter . . . even more deeply relaxed."

I heard my mind repeat "deeply relaxed" as I slumped in my chair like a rag doll. Completely limp, yet oddly more alert than before we started when my eyes were open. Geula's voice sounded as if it were coming from outer space, but her words seemed to penetrate inside me even more profoundly. "You are now on a deeper level of mind, and on this level everything is possible. . . . On this level you can experience the past or the future, or simply get information or help from the universe.

"So take a deep breath because now you are going to take a trip back in time . . . a trip back to somewhere in your past. It can be anytime in your past. However, the period of time you will see and remember will be something that was important to you . . . something that affected you then and still affects you in your life now . . . it will be something with a message in it for you that you need to know for now or for the future. Remember it and store it for your use.

"So take another breath and relax even more."

I took another breath and waited for more instructions.

Geula paused for a few moments, then began speaking again. "In a moment I will count backwards from five to one and when I reach one you will be somewhere in your past . . . somewhere that will be important to you. . . .

"Five . . . four . . . three . . . two . . . one . . ."

To my amazement when Geula reached one, inside my mind, like a slide flashed up on a movie screen I saw my grandparents' Bronx apartment with the sun streaming into the white-painted kitchen. And as I breathed in the air my nose led me to the stove and the delicious aroma of the potato knishes and fresh bread baking in the oven. I could actually feel hunger pangs in my empty stomach at seeing the food images.

Geula waited quietly while I fully experienced the sights,

smells, and feelings I was having and then continued guiding me.

"Where are you? What does your clothing look like? Who is there?"

I focused on the scene and saw my grandfather sitting next to the red-oiled-cloth-covered kitchen table holding the newspaper. I saw myself on the chair next to him. He was pointing to the words and asking me to read each one.

I was dressed in a navy-blue dotted-Swiss dress with red buttons that I owned when I was three years old.

And Grandpa, he was alive. How could that be? He had died over two years ago but there he was alive in his old rumpled black suit, talking to me. It was more than just a dream or a memory because I could clearly hear his voice and smell his special musky odor. No doubt, he was really with me.

Geula began speaking again.

"Remember," she said, "nothing comes into your life without a good reason, so record in your mind your first impressions. Look to see if there's any message for you."

Geula became silent.

And as I concentrated on the room in front of me, the thought popped into my mind that even dead people don't really die because there was Grandpa still helping me. If that was my message it was a pretty good one and it made me feel a lot less alone.

Geula waited quietly for a few minutes longer, then said, "Before we leave your past, ask for a message. Even if you don't get anything now, it's okay because you may get it later today or sometime in the future when you need it."

Geula paused again, a longer pause this time, then began again. "Are you ready to leave your past and take a trip into the future?"

I nodded, still holding onto the last of my grandfather.

"Good. Keep your eyes closed and continue breathing, deeply and evenly. . . .

"And as you breathe, you notice you are walking along a winding path . . . it is your life's path . . . and as you follow it, this path goes uphill . . . the climb is steeper and steeper . . . this path is covering not only distance but also time. You are moving to somewhere in the future. It can be as soon as tomorrow or as far into the future as fifty years."

Geula paused, waiting for me to take it all in, then went on.

"You are there now, somewhere in your future experiencing something in your life at this time. Look around you. What are the surroundings? . . . What's happening? Just let whatever comes to you come. Know you're not making it up and remember everything. Trust it's information that you need, maybe for now or for later on. . . ."

I concentrated hard on the scene in front of me and saw a school auditorium. The curtains were burgundy-colored velvet, pulled back to reveal a stage. And on the stage was me as an adult. I was holding a microphone and excitedly talking to a roomful of people. The only other thing on the stage besides me was a small oak table stacked high with books. All the same one.

"It looks so real," I said aloud, staring even harder at the scene. "But it can't be."

"Oh yes it can," Geula answered quickly. "Wait, we'll talk. Just store it all in your mind."

I recorded every last detail, even the cover of the books, while Geula waited for me. Then she began again.

"It is now time to return to the present . . . back, slowly back . . . back into this room . . . remembering everything. . . . In a moment you will open your eyelids, be wide awake and alert . . . back to the present. . . ."

Geula paused. "When you are ready, you can open your eyes, fully awake, remembering everything you experienced."

I opened my eyes, and stretched and blinked to adjust to the room around me.

"Geula, I can't believe this whole thing. Maybe I was making the whole thing up."

Geula leaned forward. "And maybe you weren't. Now, tell me what you saw."

"Well, when you told me to go into the past, I went to my grandparents' apartment. But it wasn't from now because I saw myself wearing a dress from when I was three. And my grandpa was teaching me to read and he's been dead for over two years."

Geula was nodding the whole time I was talking, then asked, "And since nothing comes into our minds without a good reason, what reason or message did you get from your visit?"

"I think . . .," I replied hesitantly, "the message that the reading my grandpa did with me was very important, and that even though he's dead, somehow he's still helping me. But I don't exactly know how. Could that be right, Geula?" I questioned.

"It could be," she quickly answered. "Let's check it out for accuracy. When I asked you what the message might be and you answered me, where did that answer come from?"

"I didn't have to think about it, Geula," I replied, now very sure of myself. "It just came into my head and I knew it was right all over my body as I was saying it."

"Yes! That's it," she said, nodding approvingly. "It sounds to me like you just got a message from the past. Good. Now, let's check out your future message. Tell me everything you saw."

"Well, that was even weirder," I answered, still seeing the picture strongly in my mind. "I saw myself as a grown-up on the stage of some auditorium. Lots of people were listening to me talk. And there were books stacked up on a small table. All the same one."

Geula listened, then said, "That's very interesting. What do you think all that means?"

I paused and looked down at my lap. "I'm not really sure. Could it be a message about my purpose, you know like Carly's supposed to be a handmaiden?"

As I glanced up, Geula had a smile on her face.

Suddenly the smile faded, as her mood changed to serious.

"Do you remember the first time after we did the 'God bless' exercises and you questioned me on how I knew you were coming?"

I nodded.

"And I told you on that morning when you got that urge to follow that path and found me, I also got a message that you were coming?"

I nodded again.

Geula paused momentarily, then said, "Well, what I didn't tell you was that I heard a voice telling me that it was very important for me to teach you as much and as quickly as I could because our time together would be short. And," she weighed each word as she looked into my eyes, "that I was to continue throughout your life."

A chill shot through my body, and we stared at each other in silence.

Geula took a breath. "Only now, hearing about the image you saw in your future, do I realize what your purpose is." I nodded as she spoke. "It is to share all that I've taught you and will continue to teach you, with as many people who will want to listen to get the help they need."

My stomach knotted up in panic at the idea of people learning from me. I felt pressured to fulfill this huge task Geula had just given me and terrified that I wouldn't be good enough.

"I'll never be able to talk like you can, Geula," I pleaded desperately. "I don't care what my future image showed. No one is going to want to listen to me." Then I added, "Besides I'm not anyone special for them to pay attention to. I'm just an ordinary person."

Geula smiled. "I'm afraid you're not getting off the hook so easily. The reason you've been chosen for this purpose is precisely because you are an ordinary person. Only an ordinary person who has experienced the same joys and struggles as they have will be listened to and trusted."

Then Geula looked at me with more love in her eyes than I had ever seen there before.

"You know, honey, teaching others isn't only giving them knowledge, it's who you are. Who you are as a person, your caring and desire to help, is the message." Geula reached over and touched my hand. "Even at this young age, you are well on your way to affecting others. I have already seen how you have cared for and influenced Carly and my Mariel, and I'm sure many other people that you're not even aware of.

"So when you grow up, just continue the same way.

"And one more thing," she added. "Never, never compare yourself with others and think you're not good enough. You already are more than enough. Just be yourself, do what you're here to do, and the rest will fall into place."

"But, Geula, what will I teach?" I asked, anxious about this big job I had just been given.

Geula smiled. "Don't worry about it so much. Whatever you learn in your life, whatever fills your heart and soul, and helps you to grow and change . . . share that with others around you. All you have to do is help people to feel good about themselves as they are and to know that they can be even more than they could ever possibly imagine. Give them the insights to find who they really are inside and what matters most to them, so they can live out their purpose just the way you're going to live out yours."

"But, who will I teach?"

Geula looked at me and smiled again. "Just like you found me, others will find you. You'll see."

"I'm so scared, Geula," I replied, not feeling any better. "What if I do the wrong thing and hurt someone or ruin their lives?"

"Honey, you're a loving person," she persisted. "People who come from love can never ruin anyone's life.

"I promise, for those that come for your help the 'right' words will come out of your mouth. That 'inner knowing' I taught you about," she touched the top of her head, then patted her chest, "will have the answers. And with education and time and knowledge from all the experiences, as well as God and all the universe's spirits and all the real people that will be there to help you . . . and me, of course . . . you will know everything you need to."

"How will I know when you're there?"

Geula took my hand.

"Through all your information receivers."

"But will I actually see you again?" I pleaded.

"Sometimes," she said. "Not like this though. It will be inside as an image on your mental screen exactly the way you saw your grandfather before. There will be other ways, too, that you'll know I'm there. . . . At times, you won't see me at all, but you'll feel as if I'm around you, while at other times, you might only hear my voice speaking in your head.

"Whatever way it will be, when you need me, or when I want to give you some answer or direction, you will know it.

"Now, one more thing." Geula reached inside her dress pocket and pulled out a sealed, light-blue envelope and handed it to me. "Here, take this. Promise me that when you get home, you'll put it away for safekeeping. Will you do that?"

"What's in it?" I asked, curious about the envelope in my hand.

"It's not to be opened yet. For now, please, just put it away safely," she said, looking deeply into my eyes. "One day when the time is right, you'll know."

I nodded, not fully understanding, and shoved the envelope into the pocket of my shorts.

Geula patted my hand. "Thank you," she said quietly, then stood up. "And now it's time for you to go."

I froze in terror. "No, Geula, don't say that." I threw myself into her arms. "I can't. Not yet."

She put her arms around me while I buried my head against her dress and sobbed.

When my crying slowed down a little, Geula helped me sit up in my chair. "Come, let's walk outside and we'll talk," she said softly. She gently but firmly took my hand and guided me out the porch door to her backyard where the lawn met the path that led into the woods. I kept my head down and wiped the tears from my eyes with the back of my hand as we walked.

She knelt down on the grass, and turned me toward her so that she could look into my eyes.

"Honey, separation from someone you love is very hard. But when you love someone and you can't be with them anymore, always keep them alive in your heart and mind. Remember them in all the detail you can . . . all their words, and everything you ever shared together. Never forget any of your memories and your love. And if you do that, neither time, nor distance, nor death will ever take that person away from you."

Geula put her hands on my forearms for a few moments as we looked at each other, then said, "No matter how far away you are or how old you get, I will be here for you. Just look for a sign that I'm around. Now, one last hug and then you must go."

I squeezed Geula as hard as I could, feeling the softness of her body, and sniffed as deeply as my nose would allow to take in her familiar lavender scent. I had to remember every part of her as clearly as possible this last time.

Geula sensed my hesitancy as I clung to her. She held me tightly for a long moment, and then firmly said, "Go."

From the unwavering tone of her voice, there was no other choice but to obey.

I let go of her, turned around without looking back, and ran down the path into the woods toward the brook, the lump in my throat burning and choking off my air supply.

I fell in a heap by the side of the brook and began rocking back and forth, sobbing.

"Life stinks!" I cried out to no one. "Do you hear me? Life stinks!" The only reply was the sound of the water as it indifferently gurgled over the stones. After a while I stopped rocking and closed my eyes. Never had I felt so totally alone. Not even my move from the Bronx was as devastating as this loss.

"I need you, Geula," I pleaded, desperate for an answer.

And then it happened as she had predicted. I saw Geula as clearly as if she were standing right in front of me. With my eyes still closed, I stared harder, straining to see her better.

"Honey, life does not stink," Geula said in her familiar yet determined voice, "but there are times when it can be very painful, almost too much to bear. Sometimes things happen to us that are unfortunate, even tragic. All you can do is live through them the best way you can. And if you're sad and angry . . . that's good. In fact, it's very necessary. Allow yourself to have every one of your feelings, but don't get stuck moaning and complaining endlessly. It's definitely not okay to let your emotions get the best of you and take control over your life."

I shook my head, still keeping my eyes closed for fear of losing her again.

"It's very important to remember what I told you about blind faith and to trust that you need each and every one of your experiences, even the painful ones." She paused. "But, it's even more important to get back to your job of living out your life and your purpose . . . the reason why you're here."

Suddenly, Geula stopped talking and waited as if she were listening to someone. Then she leaned forward in my mind's image and looked directly into my eyes.

"I was just told to tell you to look for a sign today," Geula said, smiling. And as quickly as she had appeared, she disappeared. I squeezed my closed eyes tighter and strained for more of her. I waited, hoping. Nothing but darkness, like after the credits are over on an empty movie screen.

Reluctantly, I opened my eyes and looked around.

Had she really come to tell me to look for a sign or did I in my desperation make up the whole thing so that I would feel better?

What did it matter anyway? My stomach ached, like there was a huge empty hole inside and I was still all alone and miserable, without Geula.

Slumping forward I crossed my arms over my stomach and began rocking back and forth again to soothe my terrible, longing pain. And as I rocked, I found myself whispering her name out loud. Repeating it over and over, that maybe somehow the sound of it in the air would bring me comfort. "Geula, Geula, Geula."

SIGNS IN THE PRESENT

Geula, Geula, Geula . . ." The sound of my own voice snaps me out of my trance. I shake my head to clear it and look around to check my bearings. Satisfied with where I am, I go back to thinking. It never ceases to amaze me how I can actually be driving a car, and yet be somewhere else living out my life experiences. But then, Geula had taught me that we don't just live in our bodies. We can live many dimensions at once. So while one of my dimensions was driving the car, another one was back in my past talking and living out my time with Geula, while no doubt a third was getting ready for what was going to happen next.

And what was it Geula said to me in the car before I drifted back to 1944? Oh yes . . . her old familiar, "You'll know when the time is right."

If there was one thing I had learned from Geula over all these years, it was that my answers would be there when the timing was right and that didn't mean earth time either, but rather universe time. Geula has taught me that earth time was created by people so that they could organize their lives into slots and time spans. And that the only way to live your life was by universe time. That earth time had no real meaning in regard to our age or life events, and whatever happens to you doesn't happen a minute too soon or a minute too late, no matter what you think, want, or expect. "Don't try to control or think you know the answers," she would say. "Blind faith and trust. You'll know when everything is exactly in its rightful place and it's time to know. Just keep your eyes and mind open for the unexpected and wait to see what's in store for you."

"I remember it all, Geula," I think, smiling to myself.

Okay, now what else did she say? What were the last words that I heard in my head?

"Look for a sign today."

What sign could she possibly be talking about? Obviously it was a very important one for her to come to me the way she did. Her appearance was no accident.

I can feel the beginnings of a headache over my eyes, no doubt from all my trying to reason out the unreasonable. "Stop thinking so much. Just look out the window at the scenery," I tell myself. Thank goodness, one of my special abilities is to stay in the present moment and let whatever is bothering me go.

Besides, it's an absolutely perfect day and I'm all psyched up for work, especially because I'm seeing Jessie. I've been working with her since she was four years old when she was brought to me six months after her mother overdosed on drugs. Helping her over the years to heal and grow into a well-adjusted young adult, no doubt, has been as good for me as it was for her.

I turn onto Central Avenue and pull up to the front of my office building.

No way . . . I can't believe my eyes. A meter right by the entrance. "Is this your doing, Geula?" I ask aloud to no one. Not much of a sign, if this is it, I muse to myself, knowing full well it's not. I quickly put three dimes into the empty slot, check my watch so as not to get a ticket, and wave to Jessie who is patiently waiting by the door.

Instead of traditional office therapy, Jessie and I have fallen into the habit of going to the coffeeshop. It seems easier and more natural for her to open up over food.

As I approach she smiles and points to her backpack.

"Let's go into the office instead of eating today," she says quietly, her smile suddenly vanishing. "I have something very special to show you."

"What is it?" I ask, concerned by the change in her face.

"Wait, you'll see when we get inside."

"Okay," I answer back, as we walk down the hall to my office and settle into the same ritual chair positions we have been taking since she came first to me, she sitting in my chair and me in hers.

I wait in silence as Jessie reaches into her backpack and pulls out a slightly worn, light-blue envelope.

"I got this from my grandma when we visited Sunday. It's a photo and a card written by my mother, just before she died."

My eyes are riveted to the light-blue envelope as goose bumps break out all over my skin. My whole system is vibrating like I'm overcaffeinated as an excited rush is setting off every nerve ending in my body.

Jessie sits silently, toying with the envelope, then asks, "Do you want to see them?"

I nod half-listening, still staring at the envelope as my mind races backward in time to when Geula gave me that exact same type of blue envelope and told me to "put it away for safekeeping." And I did so many years ago.

Without a doubt this is my sign. I know it, not just from the appearance of the envelope, but from that absolutely sure feeling inside my body, that Geula had called my "inner knowing."

Jessie notices my changed mood. "Is something wrong, Ivy?" she asks, now looking worried.

I look up at her and smile, both to calm the concern I see growing in her and to regain my professional composure.

"Not at all. You want to hear a weird coincidence?" I continue without waiting for her to answer. "On the way here I was thinking about a blue envelope that was given to me by a special woman, and you come in with an envelope that looks like the exact same one."

"That really is a coincidence," Jessie says, suddenly brightening. I can hear the relief in her voice. "And mine's from a special woman too. My mother."

I nod, take the envelope from her hand, and open it. There in the photo is a beautiful blond young woman smiling at the little girl she's holding in her arms, Jessie. I examine the card. It's a Mother's Day card, filled with warm sentiments. Nobody looking at this picture and reading the card would believe that in less than a month, this beautiful, seemingly happy woman would be dead.

Jessie and I spend the rest of the session talking about her mother, and at the end of the hour, she picks up the precious photo and card that are on the desk, and carefully places them back in the envelope.

As she gets up to leave, I touch her arm and say, "Thank you for bringing the envelope and sharing everything with me, Jessie." We give each other our usual parting kiss, then I add, as I always do, "See you next week."

As soon as Jessie leaves, my mind quickly returns to my blue envelope, the one Geula had given to me. When she had told me to put it away safely, I did so, tucking it inside the cover of my favorite book, the Bible, written in comic book style for children.

For some unknown reason, it seemed like the right and only place for it. And there it stayed unopened as Geula had requested, over all these years. That is, up until now. Without a doubt, my sign was clearly telling me today was the day and the timing was now. I nod, reinforcing my decision.

"As soon as I get home, that's the first thing I'm going to do," I tell myself. And all around me in the room, I feel Geula's essence saying, "Yes, yes."

FOLLOWING INNER SIGNALS

Finally the last client leaves and I'm back in my car, speeding home, obsessed with reading Geula's letter.

However, I've learned from my past experiences what we plan on doing doesn't always happen. Too often what's supposed to happen instead somehow takes priority. And is usually accompanied by all kinds of signs, messages, and forceful urges that come one after the other and can't be ignored.

So even though my burning desire is to immediately rush home and open the envelope, something seems to be getting in the way. Now all of a sudden, for some unknown reason, instead of my mind being occupied with the letter, it's suddenly focused completely on Geula's name. And I find myself fixated on the strange spelling . . . GEULA. How come it wasn't spelled "Julia," like all the other Julias I had known in my life? And even stranger, why hadn't I noticed it or thought of it before, and why now with such intensity?

I've learned to pay attention to whatever is happening to me inside and out, and now find that something won't let me go home without looking up the meaning of her name, almost as if my whole being must know, now . . . as if there's no other choice.

I detour off my drive home, head straight for the library, and quickly pull the car into the library parking lot. Heading in the door, I easily make my way to the correct section as if it were only yesterday that I was there looking for baby names for my children, and reach for the exact same book, *The Johnathan David Dictionary of First Names* by Alfred J. Kolatch, as if it were an old familiar friend.

Crouching down with the book resting on my knees, I turn the pages to the girl names and to the section beginning with "G." "Germaine, Gerry, Gertrude, Geula." My finger follows the line across to the meaning. Tingles break out under my scalp and course throughout my whole body as I stare down at the page in front of me. I can hardly believe what I'm reading: "GEULA—from the Hebrew, meaning redemption, spiritual salvation, to free, liberate, save."

How can this be true? I question. Yet, without getting an answer, I know it is. Geula had said to look for a sign, but she neglected to tell me *she* was the sign.

I tenderly push the book back into the empty slot on the shelf as if I'm touching some holy book, and rush out of the library.

Driving home I'm blinded by my tears and overwhelmed by intense feelings of love . . . Geula's love for me, and suddenly mine . . . for myself, for everyone in the universe, but mostly for Geula. If only I had found out who she was before, how much more I could have learned from her and given to others. Maybe it wasn't too late to start. I had to find out what was in her letter.

Quickly I climb the stairs to my bedroom and grab for my white wicker chair. I drag it into the closet and climb up to be able to more easily rummage around on the shelf above the hanging clothes. Finally my hand touches the brown dried leaves of my comic book Bible, and as I lift it off the shelf, pieces of the brittle pages break off in my hand and fall to the floor.

Gently opening what's left of the cover, I find the light-blue envelope, a little faded and dustier than when it was first placed there. I step down from the chair, walk to the bed, and settle my back against the pillow. Carefully I lift the flap of the envelope. The glue has since dried out and it practically opens itself.

I slide out the folded pages, stare down at the handwritten words, and begin reading.

GEULA'S LETTER

My dear children,

It is time . . .

Time to take charge of your life.

Time for you to reclaim the childhood dreams that have disappeared, the specialness that you have given away, the talents that have been wasted.

It is time for you to have the life you want and the one you were meant to live.

You are not on this earth by accident. Each breath you take, each word you speak, each thought, feeling, action, impacts on everyone . . . the entire universe. In fact, just your being born has changed the course of the world forever.

You are valuable and unique. No one has your smile, your voice, your fingerprints. No one has your particular taste or style or sees things as you do. You are truly one-of-a-kind. You have been made special for a purpose and only you are qualified, so take your precious life and your purpose seriously.

"How can I?" you answer back.

"I'm too old. What purpose could I possibly have? I'm not educated enough and my current circumstances won't permit it. I've made so many mistakes and missed my opportunities. It's too late for me; this is just the way I am."

Stop immediately! None of this is true.

Oh, I know you really believe these excuses, but they're only illusions that you use to limit your potential. All your restrictions have been programmed inside from years of memories, wounds, and traumas. You have been trapped by and have been living out family and societal values inconsistent with your real self. I also know you are afraid to change, to leave behind all that has been secure and familiar to you . . . even your old patterns, habits, behaviors that have not helped you, but you know so well and have used to comfort yourself . . . to fill up the empty holes from childhood, which can never be filled. What a shame and what a waste.

You are powerful, more powerful than you permit yourself to know.

You deserve the best, and can have it, but you must do the work.

You must stop crying over the "if only's " and "should haves." Stop beating yourself up with guilt and remorse . . . hurt . . . anger.

Let it all go.

Know that your past, no matter what has or hasn't happened to you, every lost opportunity, each experience and person from your birth up to this moment, has been placed in your life to serve your evolution and to move you to NOW.

And since NOW is the only time, you can and must begin again. Begin by believing in yourself . . . in your own unparalleled personal power and unlimited abilities.

Begin by making today the first day of your new life. . . . A rebirth, if you will.

And since this is your rebirthday, I have precious gifts for you, the greatest gifts you will ever receive. However, open each one carefully and take each message very seriously. Each one separately is valuable for your daily growth. Cumulatively, they will move your life to a place you only dreamed of, but never believed you could actually have. So, if you are ready to accept and use these gifts . . . let's begin by opening each one:

The first is to let yourself OPERATE FROM STRENGTH.

Why is that important? you are thinking.

Because no matter how much you may wish or expect or believe you deserve in life, you don't get what you want, you get what you are. The way you think, speak, act, and live out your life, determines what happens to you . . . in other words, it creates your reality.

I can't create reality. It's a fact. Everyone sees the same things, you are probably countering.

That's not true. The physical world is only an illusion. It has no power over you unless you give it strength. Your perception creates the world around you. What you select to see and not see and how you decide to react to it is all up to you.

In life there is a law of cause and effect . . . karma, if you will, and what you send out is what you continue to bring back. If you expect pain, problems, rejection, and difficulty, you will see, believe, and live out only that. And sadly with those kinds of negative attitudes it becomes easy to overlook the pleasures and opportunities all around you.

Being a victim isn't circumstantial as you have been made to believe, it is choice and a mind-set.

True, when you were a child, your parents and the outside world determined and shaped the choices you lived by and the way you were taught to think, but it doesn't have to be that way any longer.

Now the power of choice is in your hands.

Now you are free to think and believe any way you choose.

And since life is a series of choices, it is important you make new ones.

You can begin your new choicemaking by first asking yourself: Is there anything that I am causing or permitting to happen to me?

What am I saying or doing to hold myself back or to deprive myself in some way?

Take full responsibility for yourself.

Look at your life the way you are living it now instead of blaming the outside.

Then start to take control by changing your mind. That means, changing the way you think, feel, and act. The way you speak to yourself about yourself, about the people in your life and about all the situations you face daily.

Next, come from a position of strength. Begin to see the people and experiences in life merely as is, neutral, without judging them right or wrong, good or bad. Just deal with whatever or whoever as a necessary experience for your growth.

Change your perception.

Live from the inside-out, because when you change your inside—your perception—the outside world and the people automatically become a whole new experience.

Change your "self-talk," the internal and external words you use on yourself.

Speak to yourself in self-enhancing ways.

Give up the old family messages and negative labels you keep attached to yourself, you hurt yourself with. Become your best supporter, your best ally, even if you don't feel it yet. Act "as if" you do, and with time it will happen.

Change the way you handle your feelings.

If you feel doubt, fear, or anxiety, or maybe hurt, anger or negativity takes over, know that's not only to be expected, but necessary for your health and growth. Simply use them all as motivational tools to strengthen you.

So, when self-doubts, or feelings of unworthiness pop into your mind, tell yourself that it's no surprise when you are courageously attempting new things and moving away from old patterns. Give yourself praise for your courage and remind yourself that you are deserving of success and having. Let yourself off the old painful "hook." Let yourself have and grow without sabotaging it or giving up on yourself.

And when any of the many forms of fear overtake you—fear of rejection, fear of failure, fear of the unknown, fear of success— know that it is just another roadblock, another way you stop yourself from outgrowing the familiar and moving forward.

When you feel any type of fear from now on, instead of letting it hold you back, remember that fear is only "false expectations that appear real." It is an illusion to be carefully examined, a new challenge to be overcome. Let all your alarming thoughts energize you. Let them move you to the very action you are scared of, yet so desperately need to take. Don't wait until you feel better, stronger. Overcoming anything doesn't come from waiting; it comes when you face it down and keep on going.

And when you feel anger, frustration, know that the emotion is healthy and shows something is important to you. See the anger as a good reason to make changes in your life or to correct something that's wrong, not as a reason to yell, attack, argue, or feel victimized, leaving you stuck in your anger so that you have no time for the bigger task—that of changing and growing.

Remember, life is not filled with problems, only a mixed bag of "tests," challenges, and help from the universe, if you will. And know that everything in the world is exactly as it should be, and it is there to serve your transformation.

So from now on, no matter what experience comes up in your life, empower yourself by asking: What is happening right now? What am I feeling? What choices can I make to effect some change? What do I need to say or do to operate from a position of self-worth and effectiveness?

Then and only then, will you be living out your natural inherent power, your true sense of self.

And to strengthen and expand your true sense of self, you need to open your second gift.

This one by itself is so powerful, it can change the life's direction of another and can heal the world. It is the priceless gift of LOVE.

It is love in all its many wonderful forms: love from and for significant others, love of nature and beauty, love for your work, and love for yourself.

You see, from the moment you took your first breath on this planet, you were meant to know love, to be loved unconditionally, to feel safe, warm, nurtured. And as necessary as it was to be loved and to love all those people in your life, nothing was or will be more important than the love from yourself to yourself.

What it means to love yourself is to honestly know and honor yourself—to be true to that unique person within you—to express the real you fully out loud so that others can know you too. Shouting to the world, "This is me, this is what I like and don't like. What I feel, believe, think. What I want."

To love yourself also means to care about and accept everything about you "as is," to love your dark side including loving all your failures, mistakes, idiosyncrasies, and shortcomings and accepting that some of these characteristics may never change. It means giving up the shame you have been carrying, and the mask you have been wearing to hide the real you from the outside world. Giving up all the judgments about your so-called unlovingness.

It is crucial to do so because every time you judge yourself unworthy of love and see yourself as not enough, you create an inner emptiness. This in turn creates an insatiable hunger for the love and approval of others, which is an unfortunate setup for being controlled, hurt, and rejected. Placing you, your life, and your self-esteem at the mercy of another.

Isn't it sad, that you are so afraid that you will be abandoned by another that you end up abandoning yourself? Just for the few smiles and kind words you crave.

You must give this up NOW.

Love is not a commodity to be bargained over or in short supply, or that you have to earn with "good" behavior.

Love is abundant; it is all over. And the more you trust and feel love around you, and the more you feel it for yourself, the more you will see it in the world and manifest it in your life.

Remember? You get what you see and believe. So if you want love, you must make the change.

Begin by keeping your heart open, always ready to give and receive love, and know there is no reason to suffer any longer. Stop wasting time in hurt, pain, anger, rejection, fear, and "otherating."

Stop forfeiting yourself for the few crumbs that are doled out to you.

Work on your feelings of deserving, as is, regardless, because the more you give yourself the love and whatever else you deserve, the more you'll be deserving.

If you want love and approval, look to yourself.

If you want answers, look to yourself.

Trust and love your ideals, your values, your dreams, unconditionally.

It is your life, go after what you want. Don't sit and wait for someone to hold your hand or give you permission. You may wait forever.

Be there to love yourself through every experience, no matter what the outcome. Paradoxically, only when you truly love yourself and don't need another's love and approval will you finally win it and, more importantly, their respect.

And if you don't get it, you will ALWAYS have your own.

And as awesome as it is to love yourself, to fully live in love in its most magical sense is to experience the many ways to LOVE OTHERS.

Just as you are shaped by love, others are too. That's why it's so very necessary to see the best in everyone. To look for their inner beauty and the specialness that is inside each person. Just like it's important with self-love to care about and praise yourself, it is equally important to give that to others. To give them the recognition that they truly deserve and need so badly. To give appreciation, encouragement, affection. To smile at them, to nod, to wink, to laugh with them, to touch their hears and souls, and to listen. Listen for their fears, their joys, their concerns, no different than your own.

Understand and have empathy for their humanness, their limits and shortcomings, and see them in a flexible, accepting way. And no matter what the situation, even when you are angry, take time to wait so that you act and not react. Remember, words are powerful, so use them well. Then come from love. "Accent the want, not the fault." Gently tell what you want and like, not how "bad" they are and what they did wrong.

In love there is no room for attacking or fault-finding, there is only room for expressing yourself and caring—caring for yourself and caring for the other.

"I feel this way when you do that." Then let it go. Don't hold onto the anger, hurt, or pain. It will only rob you of your energy, energy that you need to live fully and to stay in love.

And now that you are operating from strength and living in love, you are ready for your third gift.

This gift is more incredible than you can imagine. In it lies your future, your happiness, and the potential for living your life on purpose. Finally living the life you want, the one you were meant to live.

It is the gift of BEGINNINGS AND ENDINGS, the cycle of birth and death and birth again. The rebirth of the real you.

You see, all of your life, from the time you were born, has been about beginnings and endings. Some were small, even insignificant or taken for granted: changes in the weather, the seasons, days, and years. Others were crucial lifetime events: leaving the comfort of home for your first day at school, graduation, moving out on your own, a job change, divorce, illness, retirement, aging, the death of someone close to you.

There were endings with new beginnings that you tried to avoid, denied, refused to accept, raged over, cried about, mourned, and grieved. Some you may remember as if it were yesterday, others you are still living with, feeling the pain and fear of impending loss or change.

And yet in each ending and beginning is held the potential for your life, both full and empty at the same time, this time of darkness and unknowing for you.

But like the phoenix rising out of the ashes, with each ending, each loss, a new phase of your life is born. A new beginning of personal growth and direction is taking place.

And although endings are sad, often confusing, and painful, only with them can miracles take place. Often something that you couldn't have imagined or predicted yourself.

Only by accepting the inevitability of endings can you begin your life anew.

Only with endings can you give birth to a higher, more evolved you. Without endings you will be stuck, stagnant, simply existing. By not accepting change and endings, you will continue living out the same old, same old. You will age, but you will never grow. You will die before you have ever really truly lived.

And whether you choose it or not, endings and change are continuously occurring in your life and all around you anyway. So since they are, why not accept them with open arms . . .

Leap empty-handed into the void—that place of transition between the end and before a new beginning has yet formed. . . .

Know that whatever is happening, both inside and out, is serving your evolution, even if you don't know what it is. And although it isn't comfortable, most always is lonely and scary, just know that whatever is going on, the forces of the universe are at work in your life, waiting to bring you the miracles that are there, waiting for you to do your part.

However, what is required of you is an act of courage while you live in this unsure space, a leap of faith.

Be willing to look closely at what you're holding onto, old attitudes, habits, mind-sets, that no longer serve the new, evolving you. Accept everything that's taking place, and don't judge what should or shouldn't happen . . . you don't know the reason so don't try to figure it out.

Instead, trust any insights, any visions that come, then let yourself and your life shift and move . . . let all the obstacles of your past and your endings be the gateway that will lead you to new beginnings.

Accept your transformation.

Welcome the endings. Welcome whatever the new beginnings have in store for you because then, *and only then*, will you truly be living out your life, fully and on purpose.

And now for the last and smallest gift. And although seemingly insignificant, this one has the potential that with just a single new action can permanently heal what has up to now tormented you. It is the gift of GOING FULL CIRCLE.

What does that mean? you wonder.

Do you remember a time when you made an unfortunate decision or said something you regretted, and felt remorse or guilt about it and wished, "If only I could do it over again, it would be so different this time."

Well, by GOING FULL CIRCLE you get that chance. A chance to reexperience something similar in a new situation. You see, the power of the universe is always forgiving, always loving, and sees you as perfectly imperfect . . . in a state of continuous learning and healing. And because inside you don't want to do wrong, and do want to feel good about yourself, you will be given the opportunity to correct some past decision or behavior. Oh, it will never be exactly the same situation as the original, but know you will get a new one equally as valuable. And as you successfully handle the current situation in the way you would have liked to have chosen the first time, you will finally be able to put to rest the old one. Finally be able to put closure to what has been haunting you and causing pain.

You have been given another chance to begin your life again, this time with all your precious gifts to help you—operating from strength, living in love, going full circle, and welcoming endings—and knowing that with each new beginning, you are co-creating with the universe.

Today you have been reborn—all that you want, all that you

are, your true self, your natural genius, all your infinite abilities—are inside waiting . . .

Your being here today, this moment is no accident. You are here for good reason. But now, as in the past, your destiny is in your hands. Your life will be up to you.

And as you go through each day making choices, remember you are not alone and never have been.

As always, I will be here for you—to guide you, to protect you, and to love you.

Just look for a sign.
Geula

ENDINGS AND BEGINNINGS

The letter drops from my hand as tears run down my face.

"What do you want from me, Geula?" I ask out loud. "Your letter said that for all of us, this is the first day of our new life. I know you mean me also, but what do you want me to do, that I haven't done yet? How can I live in a new way?"

And inside I silently hear Geula's words.

"Remember that future image you had the last time we were together, the one where you were on a stage, with a table of books and the room was full of people?"

I nod, listening for more.

"That time is now. Share my letter with those who want to change. Talk to them and write that book you saw on the table. If you do what I ask, your new life and your purpose will be the same thing."

Instantly, all the separate pieces from the beginning when we first met were falling into place. All finally making sense to me. Geula had said I would know when I was ready and the timing was right. And now I knew what over the years I was being readied for. It was to be her messenger and bring her words to others. And that sign from her, today. It wasn't just a sign, it was a directive.

Suddenly out of nowhere I'm determined, excited with the anticipation of the task and my new beginning. Although I can't see my future exactly, I know in my heart of hearts that it's moving precisely and purposefully in the direction that I have always dreamed of.

Geula's essence is all over the room as I make my way over to the word processor. I don't have to turn around to know that she's behind me, standing in the corner by the curtainless window, next to my father's Bible stand.

How like her to be there for my big moment. No time, no space, no years have elapsed.

"Well, Geula, any ideas on how to begin?"

And without a sound in the room, I instantly know in my mind and heart . . .

Geula has placed total trust in my infinite abilities.

And now it's time for me to do the same.

My fingers touch the keys. I begin.